AF608165

THE CATHOLIC UNIVERSITY OF AMERICA
CANON LAW STUDIES
No. 119

THE GENERAL NORMS *of* DISPENSATION

AN HISTORICAL SYNOPSIS
AND COMMENTARY

A DISSERTATION

Submitted to the Faculty of Canon Law of the Catholic University of America in Partial Fulfillment of the Requirements for the Degree of

DOCTOR OF CANON LAW

BY

EDWARD M. REILLY, A.B., J.C.L.
Priest of the Archdiocese of Philadelphia

THE CATHOLIC UNIVERSITY OF AMERICA PRESS
WASHINGTON, D. C.
1939

NIHIL OBSTAT:

VALENTINUS T. SCHAAF, O.F.M., J.C.D.,
Censor Deputatus.

Washingtonii, D. C., die XXXI Maii, 1939.

IMPRIMATUR:

✠ D. CARD. DOUGHERTY,
Archiepiscopus Philadelphiensis.

Philadelphiae, Pa., die VI Iunii, 1939.

PRINTED IN THE UNITED STATES OF AMERICA
BY THE WATKINS PRINTING CO., BALTIMORE

TO MY MOTHER

TABLE OF CONTENTS

FOREWORD

The Church fulfills, in part, its divinely appointed mission both by enacting laws and by relaxing at times the obligation of abiding by these laws. The Church establishes laws which should be conducive to the sanctification and salvation of mankind in general—whether it be of the whole world or of some particular territory; but in so universal a society, numbering, as it does, among its members, men of every class and race and country, it is to be expected that at times circumstances will arise in which the removal of the obligation of a law is more conducive to the sanctification of an individual person or of a group of persons, than the rigorous enforcement of the law would be. In such cases the Church, solicitous for the welfare of every one of its members, is wont to employ what is commonly known as dispensation.

The dissertation which follows is an endeavor to set forth the general rules regarding this legal institute of dispensation which are contained in the final title of the first book of the Code of Canon Law. Accordingly, the topical division throughout the treatise is suggested by the various aspects which are considered in this section of the Code.

The first part, which is historical, will contain a synopsis of the development of dispensation in Canon Law under these several general aspects. In other words, the first part is an attempt to show the process of crystallization of these aspects, from their beginning down to the time when they assumed the form which they have under the present law, if, indeed, they had assumed their present form prior to the promulgation of the Code.

This historical section will be divided into chapters corresponding to the various succeeding periods of the Church's history, and the several phases of dispensation will be examined in so far as they were in evidence in each of these periods. The choice of periods in which to make such an examination is more or less arbitrary. But the one contained in the present thesis is made because, although all the phases under consideration do not show a marked development in all the periods, some of them give evidence of development. An added reason is to be found in the fact that, so far as canonical science is concerned each of the periods shows a particular characteristic, because of which the doctrine of dispensation in that particular period should be especially examined as distinct from the doctrine of dispensation in the other periods.

The second part will be devoted to a canonical commentary on the present law, as it appears in the above mentioned section of the Code.

As the title suggests, the present dissertation is concerned with general norms. Particular norms are included only incidentally when they are required for the correct understanding of the general norms. Likewise outside the scope of the present treatise—except when the clear exposition requires their inclusion—are those other considerations which directly concern some other institute and only in an indirect way touch the institute of dispensation as such, for example, the laws regarding rescripts. If, as a matter of fact a dispensation is granted by means of a rescript the laws governing rescripts must, of course, also be observed. Finally, the present study is not concerned with similar institutes which may exist, or may have existed in the legal system of any civil government.

The author takes this opportunity to express his appreciation to all who aided him in the preparation of this dissertation.

THE GENERAL NORMS OF DISPENSATION

ABBREVIATIONS

AAS.—Acta Apostolicae Sedis.
ASS.—Acta Sanctae Sedis.
Fontes—Codicis Iuris Canonici Fontes.
MGH.—Monumenta Germaniae Historica.
MPG.—Migne, Patrologia, Series Greca.
MPL.—Migne, Patrologia, Series Latina.

CHAPTER I

PRELIMINARY NOTIONS

Article I. Definition

Canon 80. Dispensatio . . . legis in casu speciali relaxatio . . .

The term "dispensation" in the science of Canon Law possesses a very limited significance. At present it is used only to signify an act of a lawful superior or his delegate, by which, for a reasonable cause, the obligation of a law is removed in a particular case. As will be shown later, this precise concept was not always present. On the contrary, at one time the term signified any exception from the law.[1]

The effect which a dispensation produces is not one of removing the law. On the contrary, the law remains in force, but by reason of the dispensatory grant the obligation of the law in the particular case ceases for the person or persons who are included under the terms of the dispensation. For all other subjects who are within the scope of the law in question the obligation continues.

The phrase *in casu speciali* does not mean that the relaxation must be made in favor of an individual person and from a law which establishes a single obligation. Rather, it would still be considered a "special case" if a law with successive recurrence were relaxed, and also if the law, whether of single or recurrent obligation, were relaxed in favor of a particular person (physical or moral), or in favor of the whole community, provided, in this last instance, that it be a temporary relaxation.[2] Otherwise it would be an abrogation of the law, which is distinct from a dispensation, as will be seen presently.

It is essential to the concept of a true dispensation that it pro-

[1] Brys, *De Dispensatione in Iure Canonico,* Brugis: Beyaert, 1925, p. 16..

[2] Maroto, *Institutiones Iuris Canonici* (3 ed., Romae: Commentarium pro Religiosis, 1921), 1, 361.

ceed as an act of jurisdiction from a competent superior or his delegate. For, just as a law is binding only because it is an enactment of a competent legislator, so an act which removes the bond must emanate from someone who is jurisdictionally competent to grant such a relaxation. In this regard, it is immaterial whether the grantor acts by reason of competent jurisdiction proper to himself or his office, or merely by virtue of authority and power which have properly been communicated to him.

As a sort of corollary to this last consideration mention should be made of another essential requirement, namely, that the law must be one which is dispensable. At this point it will suffice to state that no human authority can dispense from the Divine Law, whether it be natural or positive. Moreover, some purely ecclesiastical laws are relatively indispensable because, as a matter of fact, dispensations contrary to them are rarely or never granted, although as a matter of principle every human law can be relaxed.[3]

Finally, a distinction must be made between the concept of dispensation and several other institutes which resemble dispensation in one aspect or another but which are fundamentally different from it. These are:

a) *interpretation,* whether authoritative or merely doctrinal, which places certain cases outside the obligation of a law. This is a declaration of the restriction of the law and not a relaxation of its obligation.

b) *absolution* from censure, which is a judicial act performed in accordance with law.

c) *epikeia,* which is a benign and equitable interpretation of the purpose of the legislator (not of the law), who is presumed to suspend his law when an extraordinary case arises in which the strict observance of the law might result in something unexpectedly harmful or very exceptionally burdensome.

d) *permission,* or the consent of some superior, which the law requires for certain acts performed by subjects.

[3] Suarez, *Tractatus de Legibus* (Parisiis, 1856), VI, c. 12, n. 5.

e) *dissimulation,* by which a superior seems to overlook the transgression of a law in order to avoid a graver evil, without, however, removing the obligation of the law.

f) *abrogation, obrogation* and *derogation,* which take away the law itself either wholly (abrogation and obrogation) or partially (derogation).

g) *privilege contrary to the law.* For while both dispensations and privileges contrary to the law have the similar effect of freeing their recipient from the obligation of the law, the privilege constitutes a special objective norm of action which is substituted for the common law from which it derogates. A dispensation, on the contrary, grants freedom from the obligation of the common law in a merely negative way by relaxing the law in question, without establishing any private norm to take the place of the common law which is relaxed.[4]

Article II. Division

In the exposition of the general norms of dispensation which follows, the term "dispensation" will at times be qualified, and the evident implication will be that the particular point under consideration is concerned only with one or the other phase of dispensation. Accordingly, it will be well to state here the principal divisions of dispensation—which divisions will, at the same time, serve to explain the qualifying words when they occur.

A dispensation is:

a) relatively *necessary, free* (voluntary) or *prohibited* according to whether very weighty causes (e. g., the avoidance of grave scandal), merely sufficient causes (e. g., the petitioner's merits), or no just causes are present to warrant the relaxation of the law.

b) *total,* if the entire obligation of the law is taken away; *partial,* if the dispensation frees the recipient from only a part of the obligation.

c) *explicit,* when the superior shows his dispensatory will in

[4] Michiels, *Normae Generales Juris Canonici* (Lublin, Polonia: Universitas Catholica, 1929), II, 327.

clear and manifest words or signs which directly express the dispensation; *implicit,* when it is granted through signs or other facts which surely but only indirectly indicate the superior's will to dispense.

d) *single,* if it relaxes a law which has a single obligation, or if for one occasion it relaxes a law the obligation of which recurs at intervals; *multiple,* if several dispensations are given as one, for example, a dispensation from multiple consanguinity; *"recurrent",* if for more than one occasion it relaxes a law the obligation of which recurs at intervals.

e) *personal,* if it is granted directly to a person; *real* (local), if granted directly to a place and indirectly to the person in that place; *mixed,* if granted in such a way that it is shared alike by all who are actually dwelling in a certain territory and by the subjects of that territory who happen to be temporarily absent from it.

f) *temporary,* if granted for a definitely designated number of days, weeks, or months, or if it is otherwise indirectly limited temporally, as when a dispensation is granted as long as a certain condition prevails; *permanent,* if no limitation of time is made.

The other divisions, such as valid and invalid, lawful and unlawful, absolute and conditioned, are clear in themselves and therefore require no further explanation.

PART I
HISTORICAL SYNOPSIS

CHAPTER II

DISPENSATIONS UNTIL THE NINTH CENTURY

Article I. Existence

In the early centuries there were few ecclesiastical laws in existence. At the same time a rigorous observance of the existing laws was the customary practice. This twofold fact obviated all general necessity of *ex professo* treatment of the subject of dispensations. The absence of such a treatment is, in turn, probably responsible for the fact that prior to the tenth century there are no texts available wherein is set forth a juridic definition of the term, even in its broader meaning.[1]

In spite of all this there is sufficient evidence in the writings of the Fathers and of the Popes and in the decrees of Councils to show that at times a more moderate course of action was pursued which differed from the customary rigorous enforcement of the existing laws. In other words, when occasion warranted it, a relaxation of one kind or another was made, but the authors did not make exclusive use of any one term to designate lessening of the rigor of the law.[2] St. Augustine (354-430) gave expression to the general theory which even then governed the practice of the Church. He said: " . . . when, owing to the serious ruptures of dissensions in the Church, it is no longer a question of danger to this or that particular individual . . . it is right to yield a little from our severity in order that true charity may give her aid in healing the more serious evils." [3] Similarly, St. Cyril of Alexandria (376-444) wrote: "For the peace of the churches and in order that they might not be separated from one another because of dissenting opinions, condescensions are use-

[1] Brys, *De Dispensatione in Iure Canonico,* p. 11.

[2] Brys, *op. cit.,* p. 15.

[3] *Epist.* CLXXXV, c. 10, n. 45—*MPL,* XXXIII, 812.

ful."[4] Again he said that at times there is "need of great moderation."[5]

Post Factum Dispensations

Many instances of mitigation are evident in several phases of the penitential discipline. St. Cyprian (210-258), writing in the name of the bishops of a synod held at Carthage, indicated an exception whereby, in spite of a former decision to deny reconciliation to penitents except after a long penance, pardon was granted sooner, so that they might be more courageous during the persecution which was then beginning.[6] In like manner, although St. Augustine wrote: " . . . it was made an ordinance in the Church that no one who had been called upon to do penance . . . should return to or continue in the body of the clergy," he admitted exceptions in the form of reinstatements because of the public harm which might result from the observance of the strict letter of the law.[7] In similar circumstances Popes Siricius (385)[8] and Martin I (649)[9] allowed similar "mercy" to be shown.

For the abjuration of heresy, when there was a question of those who lacked keenness of intellect, St. Cyril of Alexandria permitted the use of a form more brief than the one usually prescribed. In this case insistence on the rigor of the law was likely to disturb them.[10]

With regard to ordinations, legitimations amounting to relaxation of the law were made by Hilary I (465) for those who had been ordained without the metropolitan's consent;[11] by Innocent I (414) for those ordained by the heretic Bonosus;[12] and by Leo the Great (446) for those who had been elevated directly from the lay to the episcopal state.[13]

[4] *Epist.* XLIII—*MPG,* LXXVII, 222.
[5] *Epist.* LVII—*MPG,* LXXVII, 322.
[6] *Epist.* LIV—*MPL,* IV, 348.
[7] *Epist.* CLXXXV, c. 10, n. 45—*MPL,* XXXIII, 812.
[8] *Epist.* I—*MPL,* XIII, 1140.
[9] *Epist. ad Joannem Philadelphiensem*—*MPL,* LXXXVII, 153.
[10] *Epist.* LXXXII—*MPG,* LXXVII, 375.
[11] *Epist.* XVI, in *Epistolae Romanorum Pontificum* (ed. Thiel), I, 166.
[12] *Epist. ad Macedonenses*—*MPL,* LVI, 505.
[13] *Epist.* XII—*MPL,* LIV, 661.

All the foregoing examples are evidently *post factum* dispensations, although at the same time they might also be regarded as partly *ante factum* grants, since notwithstanding the fact that they were necessitated by some past event, they permitted in the future something which would otherwise have been forbidden. For example, legitimations whereby unlawfully ordained clerics received the faculty to exercise in the future the orders they had received were, in a sense, anterior dispensations, because they relaxed the law which forbade the exercise of orders to such clerics. Of greater importance, however, in this present consideration are those dispensations which were granted in order that someone might proceed contrary to the law, that is, strictly *ante-factum* dispensations.

Ante Factum Dispensations

Since the seventeenth century there have been authors [14] who contended that *ante factum* grants were not made during the early period. This claim, however, seems to be at variance with the facts.

St. Basil (370) permitted the ordination of a neophyte when the one who was being prepared for ordination was unable to undertake the labors of the ministry because of illness.[15] Upon the death of Auxentius, Bishop of Milan (c.374), dissensions about a successor arose. The people acclaimed as their choice Ambrose, as yet only a catechumen. The bishops approved this selection, whereupon Ambrose was baptized and eight days later consecrated bishop.[16] A few years later the bishops of the First Council of Constaninople (381), one hundred fifty in number, chose the as yet unbaptized Nectarius to succeed Gregory who had resigned the see of Constaninople.[17] These were relaxations

[14] DeMarca, *De Concordia Sacerdotii et Imperii,* III, c. 14, n. 5; Thomassinus, *Vetus et Nova Ecclesiae Disciplina,* P. II, lib. III, c. 24, nn. 5-20.

[15] *Epist.* CCXVI—*MPG,* XXXII, 794.

[16] Socrates, *Historia Ecclesiastica,* IV, c. 30—*MPG,* LXVII, 543; Ambrose, *Epist.* LXIII, n. 65—*MPL,* XVI, 1206.

[17] Sozomen, *Historia Ecclesiastica,* VII, c. 8—*MPG,* LXVII, 1434; Socrates, *op. cit.,* V, c. 8—*MPG,* LXVII, 578.

of canon 2 of the Council of Nicaea (325), which forbade the ordination of a neophyte.[18]

Notwithstanding the prohibition of canon 15 of the same Council which legislated against the transfer of bishops,[19] Euphronius was transferred by the bishops from the See of Colonia in Cappadocia to the archbishopric of Nicopolis in Pontus;[20] Boniface I (418-422) permitted Perigenes to remain at Corinth in Achaia as bishop, when the inhabitants of Patrae, to which see he had been appointed, refused to admit him;[21] and the Emperor Theodosius directed the bishops to appoint to the vacant See of Constantinople, Proclus, then Bishop of Cyzicus in the Hellespont, "for he had already received letters from Celestine, Bishop of Rome, approving of this election." [22]

Gelasius I (492-496) permitted the bishops of southern Italy to dispense with the interstices for ordination, in order to supply needed clerics, for the number of clerics had been depleted by famine and war.[23]

Adrian I (722-795) granted a dispensation from the law of residence to Angilram, Bishop of Metz, and to Hildebold, Bishop of Cologne.[24]

In each of these instances there is evidence that a law existed, but also that in these special cases because of particular circumstances the law was relaxed (at least implicitly).

Article II. Concept, Cause, Author and Object

Concept. An analysis of these illustrative examples shows that the term "dispensation", or its equivalent, was employed to designate in general any derogation from or exception to the law, pre-

[18] Mansi, II, 667.

[19] Mansi, II, 674.

[20] Basil, *Epist.* CCXXVIII—*MPG*, XXXII, 855.

[21] Bonifacius I, *Epist.* IV—*MPL*, XX, 760, 779.

[22] Socrates, *Historia Ecclesiastica*, VII, c. 35—*MPG*, LXVII, 818; VII, c. 40—*MPG*, LXVII, 830.

[23] *Epist.* XIV, in *Epist. Rom. Pont.* (ed. Thiel), I, 362.

[24] Cf. Synod of Frankfort—*MPG*, XCVII, 179-200; Hefele-Leclercq, *Histoire des Conciles*, III, 1060.

scinding from any further determination of whether it was made anterior to an act to be posited or subsequent to an act already posited against the law; abstracting also from the consideration of whether it was made in a general or in a particular case.[25]

CAUSE. The content of the writings from which the existence of dispensations is deducted leaves little room for doubt concerning the question of the cause required for such practical exceptions to the law. It was generally understood that there was to be present a common necessity or utility for the Church. It is true that on occasion dispensations were granted for some private good, but such a course of action met with rebuke.[26] There are also other instances in which the cause expressed might be construed as a private good, as when St. Cyril of Alexandria permitted a briefer form of abjuration, lest the penitents be disturbed.[27] It would seem, however, that all such dispensations were granted rather under the aspect of the good which would thereby accrue to the Church at large.

AUTHOR AND OBJECT. All who admit the existence of dispensations in the earliest centuries are unanimously of the opinion that during the first three centuries bishops—each for his own territory—were the sole authors of dispensations.[28] As has been stated above, there were few universal laws in existence other than the rules laid down in Holy Scripture, or the ordinances contained in the Apostolic Tradition, and from these latter it was considered unlawful to dispense. The positive legislation was confined for the most part to regulations established by each bishop for his own diocese, for example, the laws governing the penitential discipline and the qualifications of ordinands. In granting dispensations from these particular laws for a sufficient cause the bishops were justified by the very principles of jurisdiction. This was merely an exercise of power proper to their office.

[25] Cf. Brys, *De Disp.*, p. 16.
[26] Cyprian, *Epist.* LVI—*MPG,* III, 204.
[27] Cyril, *Epist.* LXXXII—*MPG,* LXXVII, 375.
[28] Thomassinus, *Vetus et Nova Eccles. Discip.*, P. II, lib. III, c. 24, n. 14; Stiegler, *Dispensation, Dispensationswesen und Dispensationsrecht im Kirchenrecht,* pp. 72-76; Brys, *op. cit.*, p. 31.

To explain the power exercised by bishops on the very rare occasions when they dispensed from a superior's law, authors have proposed various theories. Febronius said that the bishop's power was proper and moreover unlimited as to all laws.[29] Esmein claimed that the bishops' power to dispense was essentially connected with the "plenitude of disciplinary jurisdiction," which the bishops then possessed.[30] Stiegler asserts that the power was proper to them, but only in the sense that because of the existing conditions, which rendered recourse to a superior practically impossible, the power was linked to their office of ruling their respective churches.[31]

With the close of the period of persecution—about the beginning of the fourth century—a marked change occurred, which was occasioned by the more peaceful existence of the Church. The bishops of territories, which came to be known as provinces, were able to meet more easily in council and establish laws which would govern these larger territories. At the same time laws established with papal authority became more numerous. Under these developments the active subject of dispensatory power was threefold, namely, the bishops, the provincial synods and the Roman Pontiff.

The bishops, both individually [32] and united in synods, acknowledged not only the fact of papal dispensatory power, but also its superiority to their own power.[33] In certain matters, moreover,

[29] Febronius, *De Statu Ecclesiae et Legitima Potestate Romani Pontificis,* I, c. 5, n. 3.

[30] Esmein, *Le Mariage en Droit Canonique,* II, 308-312.

[31] *Op. cit.,* pp. 77-78.

[32] Cf. the appeal of Theophilus, Bishop of Alexandria (382-412), to Pope Damasus I (366-384) for ratification of Flavian's election as Bishop of Antioch in Syria—Socrates, *Hist. Eccles.,* lib. V, c. 15—*MPG,* LXVII, 603.

[33] Cf. request of the provincial synod at Corinth (bishops of Achaia) to Boniface I (418-422) to permit Perigenes to remain as bishop—*MPL,* XX, 759, footnote 2; Bonifacius I, *Epist.* IV & XV—*MPL,* XX, 760, 761, 779; also the request of the Council of Tarracona to Pope Hilary (461-468) to confirm the transfer of Irenaeus to Barcelona—Mansi, VII, 926. Pope Hilary did not grant the desired dispensation, but the request gives evi-

the Roman Pontiffs claimed the exclusive right to dispense.[34]

The dispensatory power of provincial synods with regard to decrees of general councils was limited to the accidental features of these decrees. This in reality implied an adaptation of the laws to the necessities of the respective localities.

The power of bishops was more limited. For under ordinary circumstances they could not dispense even from the laws of provincial synods. This is implied in the fact that sometimes the synods granted this faculty to the bishops, as delegated power.[35] However, it is evident from what has been said above that these regulations were not always carried out in practice. For, because of the urgent necessities which did not suffer delay, provincial synods dispensed from general laws and bishops relaxed the canons of both provincial and general councils.

A further limitation placed upon the various agents of dispensatory power was the presence of laws which were not dispensable. No authentic declaration is at hand which determines precisely and completely the laws from which dispensations might lawfully be granted. But by uniting several texts which individually settle the question in part, it is possible to derive the doctrine then prevalent concerning the object of dispensations. It might be summed up as follows: a relaxation could be made in any positive ecclesiastical law,[36] provided that 1) it did not directly pertain to faith or good morals;[37] 2) it was not an evangelical precept;[38] 3) such a relaxation would not result in harmful effects for the Church.[39]

dence of the conviction not only that the Pope could grant it but also that the right to grant it was his, and not the bishops'.

[34] Gelasius, *Epist.* XIV, c. 9—*Epist. Rom. Pont.* (ed. Thiel), I, 367.

[35] Councils of: Ancyra (314), can. 2—Mansi, II, 514; Hippo (393), can. 2—Mansi, III, 919; Tours (461), can. 11—Mansi, VII, 946; *Codex Canonum Africanae Ecclesiae* (419), can. 126—Mansi, III, 822.

[36] No positive law of purely ecclesiastical character and authority seems to be excluded by Pope St. Gelasius I (492-496) in his writing (cf. Thiel, *op. cit.*, I, 362) or by Pope John VIII (872-882) in his letter (cf. *Epist.* XXXV—*MPL,* CXXVI, 854).

[37] Augustine, *Epist.* LV, c. 2—*MPL,* XXXIII, 200.

[38] Leo I, *Epist.* CLXVII—*MPL*, LIV, 1202.

[39] Gelasius, *Epist.* XIV—*Epist. Rom. Pont.* (ed. Thiel), I, 368.

CHAPTER III

DISPENSATIONS FROM THE NINTH CENTURY TO THE DECREE OF GRATIAN

One feature of the period about to be considered—roughly from the middle of the ninth century to the middle of the twelfth century—which distinguished it from the preceding era, was the appearance of methodical collections of the Church's laws. It might be called a period of partial crystallization, because in it an attempt was made to assemble the existing laws and present them in a concrete form. Widespread confusion as to what the law was constituted a serious obstacle to the needed reform which many desired. Prior to this time collections of canons had appeared; but, far from solving the difficulty, they often added to the confusion, either because they were composed merely for some particular need or because they were too faulty, containing, as they did, many contradictory and even spurious laws.

Efforts to clear away the uncertainty were made by such men as Abbo of Fleury (988-996) and Burchard of Worms (c. 1012). Their efforts resulted in more satisfactory collections, although they did not wholly succeed in avoiding some of the doubtful texts. Later, during the latter half of the eleventh century, the problem was approached even more systematically. Under the pontificate of Gregory VII (1073-1085) the fruits of the research undertaken in the libraries of Italy were the more perfect compilations, such as that of Anselm of Lucca (c. 1083), which succeeded not only in eliminating the doubtful and spurious texts, but also in bringing to light genuine texts which had not appeared in earlier collections.[1]

A further advance was made during Urban II's reign (1088-1099). Possibly because of the conflicts which continued to arise in spite of the collections already made, careful interpretation of the laws was begun in an effort to bring harmony out of the conflicts. Urban II himself furnished the initial impetus to the

[1] Cf. Hughes, *A History of the Church* (New York; Sheed and Ward. 1935), II, 319-320; Brys, *De Disp.*, p. 44.

movement. It was further developed particularly by Ives of Chartres (1040?-1116) and Bernaldus of Constance (1054?-1100), "who may be fairly considered the founders of critical jurisprudence within the Church." [2] It is not intended to imply that the earlier authors made no attempt to interpret the canons of their collections. At least some of them had endeavored to explain the laws, but the result of their efforts in this regard can scarcely be compared to the more scientific interpretations which began to appear under the pontificate of Urban II, and which paved the way for the development of Canon Law as a separate science.

From the standpoint of Canon Law the importance of these various collections was not so much that they presented a code of new laws. Their value derived rather from the fact that they were for the most part systematic restatements of the existing laws, reconstructed in a composite form, thereby serving to render the laws at once more certain and more readily accessible.

In particular, a change of importance to the historical study of dispensations was instituted during this period inasmuch as the *ex professo* treatment of the subject took the place of the passing consideration previously given to it. This was a consequence of the use made by the authors of the notion of dispensation to reconcile opposing texts.[3]

Article I. Concept and Cause

Concept. Although a considerable part of the works referred to was devoted to the question of dispensations, the authors had not yet abandoned the old and broader concept of it. They did not regard it as a separate juridic institute. For them it continued to be merely a mitigation or tempering of the law,[4] adopted as a

[2] Hughes, *op. cit.*, II, 321.

[3] Abbo of Fleury, *Collectio Canonum*, c. 8—*MPL, CXXXIX*, 481; Ives of Chartres, *Prologus in Decretum*—*MPL*, CLXI, 47, and *Epist.* CCXXXVI —*MPL* CLXII, 242; Bernaldus of Constance, *De Excommunicatis Vitandis* (ed. Thaner)—*MGH, Libelli de Lite*, II, 117.

[4] Abbo, *Coll. Can.*, c. 8—*MPL*, CXXXIX, 481; Goffridus of Vendôme, *Libellus V [ad Calixtum Papam] qualiter in Ecclesia dispensationes fieri debent* (ed. E. Sackur)—*MGH, Lib. de Lite*, II, 693; Bernaldus, *op. cit.*, —*MGH, Lib. de Lite*, II, 117, 141; Ives, *Epist.* CCXXXVI—*MPL*, CLXII, 242.

temporary provision against greater evils,[5] which provision should end with the cessation of the cause on account of which it was made.[6] It was, moreover, a means which not only could but should be employed when circumstances warranted it.[7]

The foundation on which these authors based their justification for such departures from the customary "rigor" of the law was charity and the provision for the utility of the Church.[8]

CAUSE. During this period fact differed somewhat from theory on the question of the cause required for dispensations. For, while *de facto* grants were made for private causes, authors almost unanimously continued to refer to dispensations as a means of providing for some *common* necessity or benefit (*utilitas*) either of the Church in general or of many persons.[9] Unanimity was lacking by reason of the fact that Algerus of Liège (c. 1106), in enumerating the causes for which dispensations could reasonably be granted, mentioned some—for example, personal qualities—which were evidently of a private nature.[10]

Brys interprets Abbo of Fleury as claiming for a legislator the right to dispense because of the "frailty of men." [11] The passage to which he refers,[12] however, appears to be an enumeration, not

[5] Ives, *Prologus in Decretum—MPL,* CLXI, 48.

[6] Ives, *Prologus in Decretum—MPL,* CLXI, 53: " . . . quod necessitas pro remedio reperit, cessante necessitate, debet utique cessare pariter quod urgebat." Goffridus, *loc. cit.*

[7] Anselm of Lucca, *Anselmi Collectio,* II, c. 33 (ed. Thaner), p. 89; Goffridus, *loc. cit.;* Bernaldus, *De Excommunicatis Vitandis—MGH, Lib. de Lite, II,* 140.

[8] Ives, *Epist.* CXC—*MPL,* CLXII, 196; *Epist.* CCXIV—*MPL,* CLXII, 218; *Prologus in Decretum—MPL,* CLXI, 58; Abbo, *Coll. Can.,* c. 8—*MPL,* CXXXIX, 481; Bernaldus, *op. cit.,* p. 117.

[9] Abbo, *Coll. Can.,* c. 8—*MPL,* CXXXIX, 481; Burchardus, *Decretum,* I, c. 77—*MPL,* CXL, 569; Ives *Prol. in Decr.—MPL,* CLXI, 52; Bernaldus, *De Statutis Ecclesiasticis Sobrie Legendis— MGH, Lib. de Lite,* II, 157.

[10] *Liber de Misericordia et Justitia,* Pars I, cc. XI-XIV—*MPL,* CLXXX, 863.

[11] Brys, *De Disp.,* p. 44.

[12] Abbo, *Collec. Can.,* c. 8—*MPL,* CXXXIX, 481: "Non enim omnis inventio necessitatem comitatur, ut alio modo fieri impossibile sit quod aliquis utiliter invenit, sicut in concilio Africano plura tractat Osius Cor-

of possible reasons for granting dispensations, but of considerations which are to be taken into account when there is a question of establishing a law. The reason for thus interpreting Abbo's words is the following: he is speaking of those things which constitute the matter of *useful* legislation as contrasted with that which is absolutely necessary; and because it is to be only useful he says that the circumstances of the particular place for which the law is to be established should be considered. A somewhat similar passage is found in St. Augustine, which is an instruction on the question of his *modus agendi* in regions where customs vary.[13]

In the writings of Ives of Chartres and of Bernaldus of Constance expressions occur such as "Utilis et honesta compensatio"[14] "probabili ratione",[15] and "rationabilis causa",[16] which of themselves and alone might be interpreted as indications that these authors were defending the sufficiency of a private good as a cause for lawful dispensatory grants. From their frequent reference, however, to the presence of some common necessity or advantage it seems logical to conclude that none but a common good to be derived would be regarded by them as a reasonable compensation for the relaxation of a law. On the other hand, it is possible that such expressions are an indication of the changing discipline.[17]

Article II. Object and Author

Object. Among the more important "collectors" whose works appeared before that of Ives of Chartres, apparently only one of them, Bonizo of Sutri, formulated an express rule determining the

dubensis ad placitum, quae libenter suscipit Ecclesia pro verissima institutione canonum. Unde considerandus est terrarum situs, qualitas temporum, infirmitas hominum, et aliae necessitates rerum, quae solent mutare regulas diversarum provinciarum. Potestate etiam multa mutata sunt pro communi utilitate ecclesiarum, quae nemo reprehendit fidelium . . ."

13 Augustine, *Epist. LIV—MPL,* XXXIII, 200.

14 Ives, *Prologus in Decr.—MPL,* CLXI, 52.

15 Ives, *Prol. in Decr.—MPL,* CLXI, 58.

16 Bernaldus, *De Excom. Vitand.—MGH, Lib. de Lite,* II, 141.

17 Brys, *De Disp.*, p. 50.

laws over which the Pope could exercise dispensatory power. He regarded as dispensable—in as much as they were not directly connected with the salvation of souls—those laws which were not concerned with faith, the sacraments, or the love of God. The canons referring to these three points were "necessary" and therefore not dispensable.[18]

Bernaldus of Constance implied that the Pope's power to dispense extended to all ecclesiastical laws when he said without qualification that the "Roman Pontiffs have always had the power to dispense the canons. For they are the authors of the canons." [19]

Then Ives of Chartres, evidently borrowing his teaching from St. Augustine,[20] proposed a classification of dispensable laws which was accepted by other contemporary authors. In the prologue to his *Decretum* he divided precepts into two classes, namely, those which are *mobiles* and those which are *immobiles.* The latter, from the infraction of which spiritual death ensues, are sanctioned by the eternal law and accordingly admit of no dispensations. Such are, for example, those which oppose vice. The former, however, which have been freely instituted to safeguard ecclesiastical discipline and to render the gaining of salvation more secure, are ordinances from which dispensations may be given. The laws governing the transfer of Bishops would exemplify this class.[21] In another part of the prologue to the *Decretum* he placed evangelical and apostolic precepts in the category sanctioned by the eternal law.[22]

AUTHOR. In accordance with the growing insistence on the notion of authority centralized in the Roman Pontiff—noticeable especially during the period of reform—there arose an almost universal recognition of the Pope as the principal active subject in whom the power to dispense resided. With one exception, all

[18] Bonizo, *Liber de Vita Christiana* (1089-1095), cited by Brys, *De Disp.*, p. 45.

[19] Bernaldus, *De Excom. Vitand.—MGH, Lib. de Lite,* II, 140.

[20] Augustine, *Quaestiones ex Novo Testamento,* q. 60—*MPL,* XXXV, 2257.

[21] *Prol. in Decr.—MPL,* CLXI, 50-51.

[22] *MPL,* CLXI, 58.

of the authors who wrote on the topic defended the right of the Roman Pontiff to dispense from the general laws of the Church. At the same time they did not speak of the dispensatory power of bishops, or they referred to it only in a general way.[23] The one exception was Hincmar of Rheims (806-882), who maintained that the Pope, inasmuch as he is the guardian of the canons, cannot dispense from the laws of general councils.[24]

Brys also cites Burchard of Worms as an exception, stating that he also supported the contention that the Pope may not derogate from the decrees of general council.[25] This, however, seems to be inaccurate, since in his *Decretum*[26] Burchard says that it is lawful for the Apostolic See to transfer bishops when some common necessity or utility is present. The law from which such a transfer would have been a derogation had been promulgated by a general council, namely, that of Nicaea (325).[27]

Further evidence of this papal prerogative is found in the practice followed by the majority of bishops, of referring petitions for dispensations, at least in the more weighty matters, to the Holy See.[28]

Although it was generally acknowledged that the power to dispense resided principally in the Roman Pontiff, and although it is true that as early as the sixth century the Popes had begun to reserve certain dispensations to themselves—which reservations became in time quite numerous—apparently not even the Popes themselves claimed that they alone, to the exclusion of all others, possessed this power. At times, various Popes censured bishops for granting dispensations, but these reproofs did not constitute a

[23] It is to be noted, in this connection, that there is question not of a bishop's own laws, from which he could dispense, but only of the common laws of the Church.

[24] *Epist.* III *ad Synodum Suessionensem*—*MPL,* CXXVI, 50; Brys, *De Disp.,* p. 44; Stiegler, *Dispensation,* p. 321.

[25] *Op. cit.,* p. 44.

[26] Lib. I. c. 77, *De Mutatione Episcoporum*—*MPL,* CXL, 569.

[27] Can. 15—Mansi, II, 674.

[28] Thomassinus, *Vetus et Nova Eccles. Discip.*. P. II, lib. III, c. 26, nn. 1-2; c. 27, n. 2.

declaration that the bishops were devoid of all power to dispense. They were directed against those who were exceeding their powers by granting dispensations which had definitely been reserved to the Holy See.[29]

At the same time the practice, followed by many bishops, of granting dispensations which were not reserved to the Holy See shows that they considered themselves as empowered to dispense when the right to do so was not expressly denied them; and Bernaldus of Constance indicates that this conviction was not entirely unfounded.[30]

In addition, many bishops relaxed laws by reason of the ample faculties granted to them by the Roman Pontiffs. Urban II (1088-1099) and Paschal II (1099-1118) were very liberal in this regard.[31]

Another item pertaining to the author of dispensations is the consideraton of the frequency of the use of this power. During this period, as a result of the reform, dispensatory power was exercised much more frequently, especially with reference to ordinations and the legitimation of ordinations.

A serious consequence of such evil practices as simony and lay investiture, at which the efforts of reform were directed, was the

[29] Brys, *op. cit.*, p. 65.

[30] *De Excom. Vitand.—MGH, Libelli de Lite,* II, 141: "Sed et alii episcopi, etsi nullo modo, ut presul apostolicus, vel canones instituere vel jam institutos judicare valeant, aliquando tamen pro modulo suo aliqua statuta temperant, et hoc maxime in legibus poenitentium, quod etiam ipsi canones illis concedunt. Nam Nicenum concilium [can. 12] episcopis concessisse legitur, ut digne poenitentes humanius tractent et canonicam severitatem in eis aliquatenus mitigent."

[31] Paschalis II, *Epist.* LXXIV—*MPL,* CLXIII, 93: "Anselmus: . . . Peto ut per licentiam vestram possim quaedam, prout discretionem dabit mihi Deus, temperare. Quod petii a domno papa Urbano, et ipse posuit in mea deliberatione. Paschalis: . . . Quamobrem nos de religione et sapientia tua diu longeque spectata nihil penitus ambigentes, tuae deliberationi committimus ut juxta datum tibi divinitus intellectum, cum Ecclesiae cui praepositus es tanta necessitas expetit, sanctorum canonum decretorumque difficultatem opportuna et rationabili [compensatione] valeas temperare." The original text of Urban II's grant, mentioned in Paschal II's letter, is apparently not available.

presence among the clergy of many who had either been ordained unlawfully or had later lost the right to the lawful exercise of their orders. At the same time there were many worthy aspirants to the clerical state who were barred from the realization of their purpose by the existence of some impediment to the reception of Orders. On the one hand, in the case of the former class the Popes, either personally or through the bishops as their delegates, made liberal use of their power as a precautionary measure. That is to say, the dispensations whereby the lawful exercise of Orders was returned to these clerics, when it was warranted, provided for the better observance of the law in the future. On the other hand, dispensations from impediments binding otherwise worthy candidates were used as a means of increasing in the body of the clergy the number of those who would themselves try to further the cause of reform.[32]

[32] Cf. Brys, *De Disp.*, p. 63.

CHAPTER IV

DISPENSATIONS FROM THE DECREE OF GRATIAN TO THE COUNCIL OF TRENT.

One of the effects of the emergence of Canon Law as a separate science distinct from the science of theology—a development due principally to the so called *Decretum* of Gratian and the consequent study given to the *Decretum* by others— was the more detailed treatment accorded the various aspects of ecclesiastical law. Dispensation as a distinct juridic institute was no exception to this general rule. In this particular field, not only was a more specific attention paid to the phases already dealt with by the authors of the earlier periods, but other considerations were added which had been omitted in the earlier writings.

Article I. Concept

Although Gratian made reference to the fact of dispensations in the more restricted sense of modern usage, he retained the broader extension of the term.[1] Shortly thereafter the Decretist Rufinus (1157-1159) formulated a definition of dispensation which approximated the restrictions of the definition expressed in the Code of Canon Law.[2] His definition exercised a comparatively great influence on the subsequent restriction of the term to its modern limitations, but it did not effect this restriction immediately. For while some of the Decretists and Decretalists accepted in substance his definition and incorporated it into their writings,[3] there were others who continued to use the term only in its broader signification. Moreover, those who comprised the former group were not always consistent in using the term

[1] Cc. 5, 11, C. I, q. 7.

[2] ". . . justa causa faciente ab eo, cujus interest, canonici rigoris casualis facta derogatio."—Singer, *Die Summa Decretorum des Magister Rufinus*, p. 234.

[3] Hostiensis, *Summa Aurea*, lib. V, *de poenitentiis*, Rubr. *De Dispensationibus*, § 1; Joannes Faventinus and Huguccio, mss. cited by Brys, *De Disp.*, pp. 98-99.

"dispensation" in its more restricted extension. Rufinus him self, for example, described as a dispensation a change in law which had been occasioned by changing circumstances.[4] As late as the middle of the thirteenth century the term was used in the more unlimited sense of a change in the law, such as that made by Innocent III in the Fourth Lateran Council (1215), when he reduced the extension of the impediment of consanguinity from the seventh degree to the fourth degree.[5]

It is also to be noted that despite the resemblance of Rufinus' definition to the modern definition the concept which it expressed was not so limited for the Decretists and Decretalists as it is today. The Decretists, it is true, distinguished the notion of dispensation from such concepts as abrogation, obrogation, derogation (in its modernly accepted sense), from permission and toleration, but usually the concepts of privilege contrary to the law, of interpretation of law, and of absolution from penalties were not clearly distinguished from the concept of dispensation.[6] Further limition was placed on the extension of the concept by the Decretalists in general who distinguished dispensation from the notion of interpretation and by the later Decretalists who distinguished it also from the notion of absolution from penalties.[7] It is practically impossible to determine whether the later Decretalists distinguished dispensation from the concept of privilege contrary to law. Some of the statements of these authors give a slight indication that the two concepts were distinct.[8] In other passages, however, the two concepts are evi-

[4] Singer, *op. cit.*, p. 150.

[5] Bartholomeus Brixiensis (1258), *Glossa Ordinaria*, ad c. 6, X, *de consanguinitate et affinitate*, IV, 14, cited by Brys, *De Disp.*, p. 196.

[6] Singer, *op. cit.*, p. 14, (ad c. 4, D. IV.); p. 422 (ad C. XXV, q. 1); Laspeyres, *Bernardi Papiensis Summa Decretalium*, p. 271.

[7] Hostiensis, *Summa Aurea*, I, *De scrutinio faciendo*, par. 6; Innocentius IV, *In Quinque Libros Decretalium Commentaria*, c. 15, X, *de temporibus ordinationum et qualitate ordinandorum*, I, 11.

[8] Innocentius IV, *In Quinque Libros Decretalium Commentaria*, c. 54, X, *De electione et electi potestate*, I, 6; Hostiensis, *In Quinque Decretalium Libros Commentaria*, c. 27, X, *De rescriptis*, I, 3.

dently identified.[9] The difficulty of arriving at a conclusion on the Decretalists' concept in this regard is increased by reason of the fact that the apparently contradictory statements are to be found even in works of one and the same author, for example, of Hostiensis. In view of these facts the most that can be said is that, if in the opinion of the Decretalists a difference existed between dispensation and privilege, the distinction was not clear and was very imperfect.

Article II. Cause

It has been noted that during the preceding period there was a lack of agreement between the practice and the theory with regard to the cause required for dispensatory grants. While the authors had been almost unanimous in insisting on the presence of a cause of common necessity or benefit, dispensations (at least in the more restricted sense of the term) had been granted for reasons which were evidently of a private nature. This apparent inconsistency was probably attributable to the fact that those whose teachings ruled out the sufficiency of a private cause had in mind the more general extension of the concept of dispensation. Since this included such notions as abrogation and obrogation of law, it was reasonable that authors should demand something more than a private good as a reason for departing from the prescriptions of the law. It seems that the subsequent restriction of the term "dispensation" contributed more than any other cause to produce between the common teaching and the existing practice the closer harmony which arose during the period now under consideration.[10]

With the acceptance of the term "dispensation" in its newly acquired limitations authors and teachers, with few exceptions, were agreed in recognizing a private good to be gained as a sufficient cause, *provided it was just and proportionate.* Prior to that time, there had been authors—Gratian (c. 1142)[11] and

[9] Hostiensis, *op. cit.*, gloss to *certa ratione*, c. 9, X, *de privilegiis*, V. 33.
[10] Cf. Brys, *De Disp.*, pp. 118, 119.
[11] Cc. 11, 12, C. I, q. 7.

Algerus of Liège (c. 1106),[12] whom Gratian followed in this regard—whose words imply an admission on their part of the sufficiency of a private reason, but they do not convey the same certainty that the Decretists and Decretalists in general give.

John of Faenza (†1190) and Huguccio (†1210), who continued to require a common necessity or utility, were the exceptions to the otherwise universal agreement on the part of the Decretists and Decretalists that a private cause could suffice.[13] These latter, by omitting all insistence on the common good to be derived, or by citing instances of dispensations granted for reasons such as personal merits, dignity and old age,[14] gave evidence that their requirement of a just or reasonable cause would be fulfilled by one which was of a private nature.

Article III. Effect of the Absence of a Cause.

Among the further considerations, added during this period, was the question of the effect of the absence of the required cause on the validity of the dispensatory concession. Notwithstanding the universal requirement—manifest in all the stages of development—of some cause for the granting of dispensations, there is little evidence to show that prior to the thirteenth century any attention was given to the question of whether the arbitrary granting of a dispensation would affect the validity as well as the lawfulness of the concession. Huguccio seemed to have been the only Decretist who gave any clear teaching on the question, but his words concerned only papal dispensations. He maintained that, although the Pope ought not to dispense without a cause, he would none the less act validly if he did so, because the Pope "has full power to establish, abrogate and interpret the canons." [15] Guido de Baysio († 1313) cited a passage from Lawrence of Spain (†c. 1255), which can be interpreted as a similar, though

[12] *Liber de Misericordia et Justitia,* Pars I, cc. XI-XIV—MPL, CLXXX, 863.

[13] Mss. cited by Brys, *De Disp.,* p. 119.

[14] Cf., e.g., Innocent III in a decretal to Hubert Walter, Archbishop of Canterbury (1200), in c. 20, X, *de electione et electi potestate,* I, 6.

[15] Ms. cited by Brys, *De Disp.,* p. 119.

merely implicit, statement of the same opinion, in the sense that it omitted any reference to the validity of an arbitrary dispensation, while it stated that "the Pope would sin if without cause he were to permit anything contrary to the canons." [16]

In the writings of the Decretalists, however, a thorough doctrine was finally evolved which for the most part is the same as the present teaching.

Regarding episcopal dispensations granted without a just cause it was the accepted teaching that they were unlawful if they constitued relaxations of the bishop's own laws [17] and that they were both unlawful and invalid if the law in question was one established by a superior authority.[18]

Innocent IV (1243-1254) pronounced as invalid dispensations granted without an investigation of the cause (*sine cognitione causae*) by those other than the legislator. At first sight his words might appear to have applied also to episcopal dispensations from episcopal laws in such a way that they too would be invalid if a just cause were lacking. However, the qualifying phrase "to whom it has been granted to dispense" limited his declaration to those concessions which were made by reason of derived power, or, in other words, to those made by an inferior from a law of a superior legislator. That this restriction was according to the mind of Innocent IV is further established from the principle which he enunciated, in the passage just preceding the one in question, namely, that if a merely voluntary constitution was the reason whereby something was forbidden, the will alone of the legislator could be the cause for relaxing the prohibition. This proposition was advanced by Innocent IV only to prove the validity of papal dis-

[16] Guido de Baysio, *Rosarium Decreti* ad C. XXV, cited by Brys, *De Disp.*, p. 120.

[17] Innocentius IV, *In Quinque Libros Decretalium Commentaria,* c. 6, X, *de statu monachorum et canonicorum regularium,* III, 35; Durandus, *Speculum Juris,* lib. I, partic. 1, *De Disp.*, § 5.

[18] Hostiensis, *In Quinque Decretalium Libros Commentaria,* c. 54, X, *de electione et electi potestate,* I, 6; Raymundus de Pennafort, *Summa,* lib. III. tit. XXIX, § 2.

pensations from positive laws, even though they were granted without a cause, but the tenor of the words was sufficiently general to admit of application also when the legislator was a bishop.

The principle just referred to is indicative of the opinion prevalent among the Decretalists with reference to the validity of papal dispensations, namely, that the Roman Pontiff's will to dispense sufficed for validity, even without a cause, if by the dispensation a simply positive law [19] were relaxed, but that dispensations from laws other than those designated as "positive," even though they were granted by the Pope, were invalid unless a just cause were present.[20] This conviction coincides fundamentally with the opinion most commonly held by modern canonists, but for the majority of Decretalists it had a less extensive application, since they confined the term "positive law" within narrower bounds than those to which modern usage is wont to limit it. Until the time of Joannes Andreae (c. 1326) it was customary to regard the general ordinances of the Church ("those which have been generally established for the perpetual utility of the Church")[21] as outside the scope of "positive law" and accordingly as not admitting of valid dispensation without a cause.[22] Joannes Andreae rejected this distinction and included this latter kind of ordinance among those from which the Pope could validly dispense without necessarily having what would be considered a just cause for so doing.[23]

While those who considered the question were in agreement

[19] "Positive" as signifying, in general, laws of ecclesiastical origin. *Infra*, pp. 26-30.

[20] Innocentius IV, *In Quinque Libros Decretalium Commentaria*, c. 6, X, *de statu monachorum et canonicorum regularium*, III, 35; Hostiensis, *In Quinq. Lib. Decr. Commentaria*, in c. 6, X, *de statu monachorum et canonicorum regularium*, III, 35; Durandus, *Speculum Juris*, I, partic. 1, Rubr. *De Dispens.*, § 9.

[21] C. 3, C. XXV, q. 1.

[22] As will be seen in the next article, some authors denied that dispensations from these general statutes could be granted even with a cause.

[23] *Gloss* to c. 6, X, *de statu monachorum et canonicorum regularium*, III, 35.

in affirming the *validity* of papal dispensations from pontifical laws ("positive" laws until the time of John Andreae) regardless of the presence or absence of a just cause, all of the Decretalists were of one mind in asserting that a lawful dispsensation—even though papal—was dependent upon the presence of a cause to justify it. It was stated without qualification that "a dispensation is forbidden whenever there is not a just cause for dispensing."[24] Other statements which indicated the same conviction were those, which demanded not only a cause but a knowledge (at times, even an investigation) of it, or which branded the granting of a dispensation without cause as an act of reckless squandering (*dissipatio*), and refused to regard it as an act of judicious administration (*dispensatio*).[25]

Article IV. Object

In determining the object of dispensation Gratian divided laws into two general categories. The one comprised ecclesiastical laws, and over these he attributed to the Pope a universal dispensatory power.[26] The other embraced the "natural" law which is contained in the "Law and the Gospel" (Old and New Testaments) or is "defined by God and contained in Sacred Scripture,"[27] not, however, in the sense that all things found in Scripture belong to the natural law. For, while he asserted the general principle that "against the natural law no dispensation is admitted", he excluded from the scope of this prohibition "mystical" or ceremonial precepts inasmuch as they refer to externals.[28] Further, he distinguished laws established by the Apostles from the general class of ecclesiastical laws and regarded dispensations from the former (that is, from the laws of the Apostles) as unlawful.[29]

Gratian's doctrine on the dispensability of laws was followed

[24] Raymundus de Pennaforte, *Summa,* lib. III, tit. XXX, § 2.
[25] Durandus, *Speculum Juris,* lib. I, partic. I, *De Dispen.,* § 9.
[26] C. 16, C. XXV, q. 1.
[27] C. 1, D. V; c. 1, D. XIV.
[28] C. 1, D. XIV; c. 1, D. VI.
[29] C. 2, D. XIV.

in general by the Decretists and Decretalists, at least inasmuch as they, too, accepted the principle that only those which were simply positive or purely human admitted of dispensation. An analysis, however, of the applications of this general rule shows that there was a rather vast difference between Gratian's teaching and the doctrine accepted by the later Decretalists. This was a result of a gradual restriction of the term "natural law", which restriction effected changes whereby some laws which had previously been considered as "natural" (or "divine", as some called them) came to be regarded as dispensable if not "positive." Also, another change occurred in the form of a more mitigated view of the indispensability of "natural law."[30]

Rufinus explained Gratian's doctrine of the natural law and its non-dispensability by limiting it to moral precepts and prohibitions as distinct from the ceremonial ones. Accordingly, for him, the natural law comprised the law of morals (Old Testament) and the laws of evangelical or apostolic institution (New Testament).[31] To these he added apostolic laws not contained in Sacred Scripture and the decrees of the first four general councils. He attributed to them a like indispensability, admitting, however, the possibility of an exception with regard to those conciliar decrees which had been established with great rigor. These two classes of laws were conceived as occupying a position midway between the strictly "natural" and the purely human laws. For, while they were not contained in Sacred Scripture, the authority upon which they were based was nevertheless regarded as above that of the purely human laws. Thus he limited the possibility of dispensations to those laws which had been promulgated only by later authorities.[32]

The other Decretists in general made this explanation their own, although they admitted exceptions. Noteworthy departures from it, however, were made by John of Spain (†c. 1186) and Huguccio († 1210). The former, in determining the dispensable

[30] *Infra*, pp. 29-30.
[31] Singer, *Die Summa Decr. des Magister Rufinus*, pp. 16, 234.
[32] *Op. cit.*, p. 34.

laws, repeated Rufinus' words, but introduced a restrictive condition, namely, that the law to be relaxed should not be one which referred to the general status of the Church, such as that which denied to those who had been twice married entrance into the ranks of the clergy. The latter, on the contrary, enlarged the class of dispensable laws in two points. First he limited the indispensability of the decrees of the first four general councils to those canons which pertain to the general status of the Church. Secondly he admitted the dispensatory power of the Pope over Apostolic laws. This admission was apparently an effort on his part to bring theory into accord with practice, since shortly before the time at which he wrote Pope Lucius III (1181-1185) dispensed one who had been twice married from the apostolic law forbidding such a one from entering the priesthood.[33]

The early Decretalists retained the classification of dispensable laws which excluded general ordinances of the Church, the decrees of the first four general councils and the apostolic canons,[34] but later Decretalists gradually recognized these three classes of laws as positive or human, and therefore as susceptible of papal dispensation. Bartholomew of Brescia († 1258), for example, stated explicitly that the Pope dispensed from general ordinances of the Church.[35] He was followed in this by Hostiensis († 1271), Innocent IV († 1254) and Joannes Andreae († 1348), for, as we have seen, they admitted the possibility of dispensations from such ordinances, at least if a just cause were present.[36] Tancredus († 1215) and Joannes de Deo († after 1253) regarded the laws of the first four councils

[33] Brys, *De Disp.*, pp. 126, 132-133. Cf. Kirch, *Enchiridion Fontium Historiae Ecclesiasticae Antiquae,* n. 695, wherein is contained canon 17 of the *Canones Apostolorum* in which the ordination of twice married persons was forbidden.

[34] Laurentius Hispanus (1220), *gloss* to *nulla commutatione,* in c. 2, C. XXV, q. 1; Joannes Teutonicus (c. 1215), *gloss* to *apostoli,* c. 6, C. XXV, q. 1.

[35] *Gloss* to *apostoli,* in c. 6, C. XXV, q. 1.

[36] *Supra,* pp. 24-25.

as dispensable in particular instances, but denied that the Pope had the power to abrogate them.[37] Hostiensis, drawing a more logical distinction, said that the Pope could dispense the disciplinary decrees of these councils, but not those which pertained to faith.[38]

The dispensation mentioned above which Pope Lucius III had granted, and the concession of which influenced Huguccio to admit papal dispensatory power over at least some laws of apostolic origin, led Lawrence of Spain (c. 1220) and Petrus de Sampsone († after 1260) to the same conviction. Each of them, however, arrived at this conviction by a different process of reasoning. Lawrence of Spain said that the Pope could dispense because "he was possessed of a higher power than the Apostle," while Petrus de Sampsone distinguished the laws which the Apostles promulgated in the name of God from those which they established in their own name and attributed to the Pope power over the latter class.[39]

Bernard of Parma († 1263), Innocent IV, Hostiensis, and Joannes Andreae made a further distinction which advanced the development of the doctrine relative to Scriptural laws. It took the form of a more mitigated view of the indispensability of such laws. While they agreed that these precepts could not be abrogated in their entirety, they admitted that at least some of them could be made the object of a papal dispensation, for example, the law of tithes.[40]

Finally, Hostiensis divided the moral precepts of Scriptural law into 1) those which are so closely associated with the "honor of the divine majesty and the public utility of human dignity" that no substitute for them can be given, and 2) those which can be dispensed without manifest offense to God or harm to mankind. He mentioned the decalogue as an example

[37] Brys, *De Disp.*, p. 197.

[38] Hostiensis, *Summa Aurea*, lib. V, Rubr. *De Dispensat.*, § 1.

[39] Brys, *op. cit.*, p. 200.

[40] Cf. *glosses* cited by Brys, *op. cit.*, p. 202.

of the first category; the precept of tithes as an example of the other.[41]

Article V. Author

It has already been indicated that the trend of thought in the period preceeding the *Decretum* of Gratian was in the direction of a recognition of the Pope as the sole author (by ordinary power) of dispensations from the common law. Gratian and the Decretists advanced this trend without, however, expressly asserting the exclusive power of the Pope.

Gratian's principle that dispensatory power is a correlative of legislative power might be accepted as an implicit affirmation of an exclusive papal prerogative in this regard. In a sense, however, it seems to be somewhat offset by his affirmation of some episcopal power—an indefinite justification, it is true, but nonetheless a kind of defense of it.[42] In view of this the most that can be said is that Gratian enunciated the principles which were later used to establish the exclusive right of the Pope to dispense.

The Decretists proposed more clearly the exclusive papal power, although it must also be admitted that some of the Decretists' statements appear to be inconsistent with it. On the one hand, there was the frequently repeated principle of Gratian, mentioned above, (*expressly* interpreted by some as reserving to the Pope the ordinary power to grant dispensations), together with other statements denying episcopal power over the common law, for example, "They can dispense only in so far as the law permits them." [43] On the other hand, there were the apparently contradictory statements attributing to bishops some dispensatory power. These do not, however, as greatly offset

[41] *In Quinq. Lib. Decr. Commentaria,* in c. 24, X, *de decimis primitiis et oblationibus,* III, 30.

[42] C. 16, C. XXV, q. 1; c. 47, C. XVI, q. 1.

[43] Cf. Singer, *Die Summa Decr. des Magister Rufinus,* p. 423. Cf. also Summa Coloniensis (c. 1169), Simon de Bisiniano (1174-1179), Summa Lipsiensis (c. 1186), Joannes Faventinus († 1190), Huguccio († 1210), Sicardus Cremonensis († 1215), mss. cited by Brys, *De Disp.,* pp. 141, 144.

the teaching of the Pope's exclusive power as did the affirmation of episcopal power in Gratian's *Decretum,* because the dispensations considered by the Decretists to be within the bishops' power were dispensations in the broader sense (e. g., mitigation of penitential canons), rather than dispensations in the more restricted sense of a relaxation of a law. Furthermore, the delegated power which the Council of Nicaea had granted to bishops over such canons had probably never been revoked, so that the power which the Decretists attributed to them was not ordinary but delegated power.

The history of the Decretalists' teaching concerning the author of dispensations is divided into three main periods, with some overlapping, according to the power over the common law attributed to bishops in each of the three periods.

The first is that of the earliest Decretalists, who affirmed in explicit and unmistakable terms the exclusiveness of the power to dispense inherent in the Pope, and ascribed to bishops the right to dispense only when the canons permitted them to do so.[44]

The second dates from about the time of Innocent III's promulgation of the so called "Third Compilation" (1210). Speaking of absolution from penalties Innocent III said: "From the fact that the founder of the canon did not reserve to himself the absolution of it, it seems that he has granted to others the faculty to relax it."[45] Some of the Decretalists applied these words to dispensation and arrived at the conclusion that bishops "can dispense whenever the right is not denied them."[46] Others restricted this opinion somewhat by saying that bishops could dispense if simultaneously two conditions were fulfilled, namely, that such dispensations had not been forbidden and that at some time or other in a similiar case permission to dispense had been granted.[47]

[44] Laspeyres, *Bernardi Papiensis Summa Decretalium,* p. 254; Petrus Blesensis, *Speculum Juris Canonici* (ed. Reimarus), p. 45.

[45] C. 3, *De sententia excommunicationis,* V, 21—Friedberg, *Quinque compilationes antiquae,* p. 133, cited by Brys, *De Disp.,* p. 244.

[46] Laurentius Hispanus (c. 1210), *glossa ord.* ad *non retinuit* in c. 29, X, *de sententia excommunicationis,* V. 39, cited by Brys, *De Disp.,* p. 245.

[47] Vincentius Hispanus (c. 1215) *gloss* in c. 4, X, *de iudiciis,* II, 1.

In the third period, following the issuance of the Decretals of Gregory IX (1234), the Decretalists with few exceptions clearly distinguished from each other the notions of dispensation and absolution, and returned to the more logical teaching that "bishops cannot dispense unless the power has been granted to them in the law."[48] Moreover, from the time of Innocent IV (1243-1254) it was regarded as sufficient if a merely *implicit* concession was contained in the law.[49]

Finally, some of the Decretalists excepted cases of "urgent necessity and evident utility of the Church" from the embrace of the rule requiring express concession for the exercise of episcopal dispensatory power.[50]

It should, perhaps be noted here that, at least with respect to dispensations in general, an explicit concession of this power for urgent cases appeared *in the written law* for the first time when it was included in the *Code of Canon Law*.[51]

Article VI. Interpretation

The apparent absence during the preceding periods of any statement of the legal doctrine relative to the interpretation of dispensations would seem to indicate that none was considered necessary. But even in the absence of such a statement one can logically presume that, in accordance with the comparatively stricter discipline then in force, it was taken for granted that a broad interpretation could not be placed upon exceptions from the common law. Inasmuch as dispensations were less fre-

[48] Gulielmus de Nazone. (c. 1240), *gloss* to c. 4, X, *de iudiciis,* II, 1; Guido de Baysio († 1313), *Commentarium in VI°,* c. 14, I, 6; Joannes Hispanus (c. 1186), *Summa in titulis Decretalium,* tit, *De filiis presbyterorum,* mss. cited by Brys, *De Disp.*, p. 274.

[49] Innocentius IV, *In Quinque Libros Decretalium Commentaria,* c. 15, X, *de temporibus ordinationum et qualitate ordinandorum,* I, 11.

[50] Hostiensis, *In Quinq. Lib. Decr. Commentaria,* c. 28, X, *de praebendis et dignitatibus,* III, 5; Abbas Antiquus (c. 1270), *Super quinque libros Decretalium lectura aurea,* c. 28, X, *de praebendis et dignitatibus,* III, 5.

[51] Can. 81. Cf. *infra,* the concession of such power with respect to matrimonial dispensations, pp. 41-42.

quently granted, it is reasonable to conclude that, when as a matter of fact a law was relaxed, the words used to grant the relaxation would be interpreted in a restricted sense. This presumption is, in a certain sense, confirmed by the fact that the earliest statements of the Decretists and Decretalists concerning this point indicated the common opinion that dispensations must be interpreted strictly.

With few exceptions,[52] the Decretists and Decretalists proclaimed the principle of strict interpretation of dispensations, since these constitute departures from the common law. At times this principle was taught explicitly.[53] At other times it was implied in the general statements: (1) that a person who has been dispensed from one law is not thereby dispensed from similar laws or from laws concerned with matters which are of lesser moment, unless the dispensation from the one necessarily includes a dispensation from the other. For example, a dispensation from an impediment to the priesthood of necessity includes, for the person dispensed, the relaxation of the law establishing the same impediment to minor orders;[54] (2) that a dispensation may not be extended so as to include persons other than those expressly mentioned, even though similar reasons for dispensations should be present.[55]

The principle was likewise implied in their more particular doctrines relative to certain practical cases. Thus they maintained: (1) that a man who was dispensed so that he could

[52] V. g., Laurentius Hispanus and Joannes Hispanus, Mss., cited by Brys, *De Disp.*, p. 231.

[53] Raymundus, *Summa*, lib. III, tit. XIX *de filiis presbyterorum*, § 11; Hostiensis, *In Quinq. Decret. Libr. Commentaria*, lib. I, *de rescriptis*, c. 18, n. 8; Durandus, *Speculum Juris*, lib. I, partic. I, *De Dispensationibus*, § 11, n. 2; Baldus de Ubaldis, *In Decretalium Commentaria*, rubr. *de sententia et re iudicata*, cap. XIX, n. 1.

[54] Raymundus, *op. cit., loc. cit.;* Hostiensis, *op. cit.*, in c. 27, X, *de rescriptis*, I, 3; Durandus, *op. cit., loc. cit.*, n. 4; Baldus de Ubaldis, *op. cit., loc. cit.;* Panormitanus, *Commentaria*, rubr. *de clericis coniugatis*, cap. VII, n. 8.

[55] Cf. *gloss* to c. 18, C. I, q. 7; Hostiensis, *In Quinq. Decret. Libr. Commentaria*, lib. I, *de rescriptis*, cap. XXI, n. 1.

"receive orders" was thereby free to receive only minor orders;[56] (2) that a dispensation to enter one marriage did not imply a similar dispensation to enter another marriage;[57] (3) that one who was dispensed from an irregularity so that he might "retain ecclesiastical honors and dignities" could not thereby be elevated to the episcopacy "which is not only a dignity but the culmination of the dignities."[58]

Boniface VIII also referred to the general principle of strict interpretation in a decretal which contained an application of the principle. He declared that a person who had been dispensed from a defect in order that he might be promoted to a benefice "cannot on the pretext of such a dispensation (which departure from the law ought to be restricted as odious) obtain more than one benefice."[59]

Even among those who at times stated this principle unqualifiedly, there were some who in other passages proposed teachings which evidently limited the principle. Thus Raymond of Pennafort said that dispensations could be interpreted broadly if such an interpretation entailed no harm or only slight disadvantage to others, and if the dispensation, as thus interpreted, did not exceed the power of the one dispensing.[60]

Secondly, a dispensation which had been granted by the Roman Pontiff himself or by his mandate could be interpreted more broadly than a similar dispensation which had been granted by a bishop.[61]

Finally, *motu proprio* dispensations were considered as susceptible of a broader interpretation than those granted on the strength of someone's petition.[62] This opinion was based on a decretal of Boniface VIII, with respect to the conferring of

[56] Raymundus, *Summa,* lib. III, tit. XIX, *de filiis presby.,* § 11.

[57] Durandus, *Speculum Juris,* lib. I, partic. I, *De Dispensationibus,* § 11, n. 3.

[58] Durandus, *Speculum Juris, loc. cit.,* n. 6.

[59] C. 1, *de filiis presby. et aliis illegitime natis,* I, 11 in VI°.

[60] *Summa,* lib. III, tit. XIX, *de filiis presby.,* § 11.

[61] Raymundus, *ibidem.*

[62] Cf. mss., cited by Brys, *De Disp.,* p. 233.

certain prebends or dignities. In this decretal he had said that, if the favor were granted *motu proprio,* the broadest interpretation could be employed, but that, if the favor were granted in accordance with someone else's petition, it should be interpreted strictly.[63]

ARTICLE VII. CESSATION

The burden of the Decretists' and Decretalists' doctrine on the termination of dispensations was concerned with the cessation of the cause on account of which the dispensation was conferred and with cessation of the dispensation by means of its revocation.

With respect to the cessation of the cause they continually referred to the words of Leo I, which were reported by Gratian,[64] namely, that "those things which were exceptionally brought about because of the necessity of the times ought to cease when the necessity itself ceases." In their application of this principle the Decretists and Decretalists, apparently following Rufinus' interpretation of it,[65] agreed that it was not to be accepted in the sense that the cessation of the cause would bring about the cessation of dispensations which had already been granted—it was considered as "fitting that favors of superiors should continue"—but in the sense that similar dispensations should not be given after the necessity or cause had ceased.[66]

Moreover, the cessation of the necessity had to be complete in order to effect the cessation of the dispensation. For, if a reasonable utility—which was regarded as a relative necessity—succeeded the necessity strictly so called, the dispensation would not terminate.[67] Nor would the termination be effected unless the final cause (not merely an impulsive cause) had ceased completely.[68]

[63] C. 24, *de praebendis et dignitatibus,* III, 4 in VI°.

[64] C. 7, C. I, q. 7.

[65] Singer, *Die Summa Decretorum des Magister Rufinus,* p. 236.

[66] Durandus, *Speculum Iuris,* lib. I, partic. I, *De Dispensationibus,* § 11, n. 12. Cf. also marginal note to *quod* in *gloss* to *cessante,* c. 7, C. I, q. 7; *gloss* to *irritari,* c. 9, X, *de filiis presby.,* I, 17.

[67] Singer, *op. cit.,* p. 236; Joannes Andreae, *gloss* to *decet concessum,* Reg. 16, R. J. in VI°.

[68] Joannes Andreae, *ibidem.*

In the passages to which reference has been made the Decretists and Decretalists made no explicit mention of "recurrent" dispensations. On the contrary, they apparently were considering only those dispensations by which a single obligation of law was relaxed. But, despite the fact that they maintained that dispensations already granted did not cease, it seems reasonable to suppose that, in the unexpressed opinion of the Decretists and Decretalists, the termination of a "recurrent" dispensation was effected by the cessation of the cause on account of which it was granted. For, in view of the prevalent notion of dispensation as a *temporary* expedient in necessity, they would certainly have considered such a relaxation to be conditioned upon the continuance of the necessity or utility.

Concerning the revocation of dispensations the Decretists and Decretalists frequently repeated the axiom that "a dispensation, when once granted, ought not be revoked." The principle, if considered alone, might be taken as a denial on their part of the power to revoke dispensations. On the contrary, however, they intended no such denial, as will be shown immediately. Their probable meaning was that dispensations should not be revoked without cause, or else that they should not be revoked except in accordance with the rules which they proposed in this regard. They readily admitted the power to recall dispensations which had already been granted, but they placed limitations on the power, at least with respect to inferior ordinaries.

In line with their conviction that "a person ought not to contravene or nullify his own acts," they maintained that the one who had granted a dispensation could not revoke the same.[69] But they did admit that the superior or the successor of the one who relaxed the law could revoke the dispensation.[70]

It should be added, in passing, that it is not clear whether the Decretists and Decretalists, in restricting the revocatory

[69] Hostiensis, *In Quinq. Decret. Libr. Commentaria*, c. 5, X, *de clericis coniugatis*, III, 3. Cf. also *gloss* to *irritari*, c. 9, X *de filiis presby.*, I, 17.

[70] Hostiensis, *loc. cit.;* Durandus, *Speculum Juris*, lib. I, *De Dispensationibus*, § 11, n. 12.

power, were speaking of a valid revocation, or merely of a lawful one. It would seem, however, that they referred to the lawful revocation. On the one hand, the restriction of the dispenser's revocatory power was not absolute, since it was admitted that the one who granted a dispensation could also recall it if the dispensation had been granted unlawfully.[71] On the other hand, at least one of the Decretalists, Joannes Andreae, taught that "*per se* a superior (*princeps*) can lessen, change, or even remove entirely a privilege which he has granted." [72] Although it is true that this passage speaks explicitly only of privileges, it does mention the term without qualification. Accordingly, since dispensations and privileges contrary to the law were not distinct from each other in the mind of the Decretists and Decretalists, it would seem that the principle here enunciated would apply to the former as well as to the latter.

[71] Hostiensis, *op. cit.,* ad c. 5, X, *de filiis presby.,* I, 17.
[72] *Gloss* to *mansurum,* Reg. 16, R. J., in VI°.

CHAPTER V

DISPENSATIONS FROM THE COUNCIL OF TRENT TO THE CODE

ARTICLE I. TRIDENTINE DECREES

The Fathers of the Council of Trent did not devote any particular section to the statement of the general regulations governing dispensations. In several passages, however, they deemed it advisable either to repeat the already accepted norms or to enact special laws for particular instances. Thus, they restated the general attitude of the Church with respect to dispensation by declaring that it is expedient occasionally "to relax the bond of the law" and thereby provide more fully for the common good. At the same time, they indicated that the granting of dispensations is to be by way of exception; that as a general rule, the "canons are to be observed exactly by all as far as possible." They continued by saying that whenever the granting of a dispensation to certain persons is warranted by an urgent and just reason or by greater utility, they who are empowered to relax the law in question can dispense only after mature consideration of the cause.[1]

The general tenor of this passage, especially in view of the fact that no reference is made to the necessity of a public cause, indicates that the Fathers of the Council recognized in general the sufficiency of a private good to be attained. In one particular instance, however, they insisted that by way of exception a public cause must be present, that is, whenever the dispensation is a relaxation of the impediment of affinity in the second degree.[2]

Another regulation declared that dispensations which were to be sent outside the Roman Curia should be committed to the ordinary of those who requested the dispensation; and if they were granted *in forma gratiosa,* they became effective only after the ordinary, as the delegate of the Holy See, had summarily exam-

[1] Sess. XXV, *de ref.* c. 18.—Mansi, XXXIII, 192.

[2] Sess. XXIV, *de ref. Matr.,* c. 5.—Mansi, XXXIII, 154.

ined the causes and determined that the petition was not vitiated by subreption or obreption.[3]

Finally, in some instances the Fathers saw fit explicitly to communicate dispensatory power to bishops. For example, local ordinaries were given the faculty to dispense from the publication of the banns of matrimony when there was a well-founded suspicion that the marriage might otherwise be maliciously hindered.[4] Similarly, bishops received the power to dispense from all irregularities and suspensions arising out of an occult delict, unless the delict was a case of voluntary homicide or unless the matter had already been introduced in the contentious forum.[5] In another passage local ordinaries were empowered to dispense from the irregularity of homicide after the causes had been examined and their truthfulness established, namely, whenever the homicide was committed accidentally or in self-defense.[6]

Article II. Concept

The concept of dispensation as it existed in the mind of the later Decretalists was not far removed from the concept in its present acceptation. Their notion of dispensation, however, fell short of agreement with the modern concept by reason of the fact that they failed adequately to distinguish dispensation from privilege.

The canonists who followed the Decretalists saw differences between dispensation and privilege. As a matter of fact, Suarez maintains that the common opinion of his time taught a distinction between the two.[7] Yet the distinction which these authors made did not completely differentiate the two concepts. Suarez[8] himself, for example, agreed in general that dispensa-

[3] Sess. XXIV, *de ref.*, c. 5.—Mansi, XXXIII, 135.

[4] Sess. XXIV, *de ref. Matr.*, c. 1.—Mansi, XXXIII, 152.

[5] Sess. XXIV, *de ref.*, c. 6.—Mansi, XXXIII, 160.

[6] Sess. XIV, *de ref.*, c. 7.—Mansi, XXXIII, 105-106.

[7] *De Legibus,* VIII, c. II, n. 10, where he cites Mandosius and Rebuffus as proponents of this opinion.

[8] *Loc. cit.:* "Solum . . . illa dispensatio poterit privilegium appellari, quae per modum legis privatae conceditur ad operandum ordinarie, et stabilitur contra aliquod jus commune. . ."

tion differed from privilege. Nevertheless he said that a dispensation could be regarded *(appellari)* as a privilege if it was granted as a private law to be used as an ordinary norm of action and if it was established in opposition to some common law.

Apparently it was only about the time of Reiffenstuel and Schmalzgrueber—that is, during the late seventeenth century—that the two concepts were completely separated from each other. Although there were authors of the same period who identified privileges contrary to law with dispensations[9] these two canonists clearly and adequately distinguished one from the other, thereby completing the development of the concept of dispensation.[10] Since that time the term has been employed in the restricted sense which present day usage attaches to it.

Article III. Author

During the age of the later Decretalists the principle had been firmly estsablished that inferior ordinaries could not dispense from the Church's general laws unless they had been given the power to do so either explicitly or implicitly, or unless there was present an urgent necessity and evident utility of the Church. This doctrine had apparently approximated the present law of the Code. Between the time of the Decretalists and the publication of the Code, however, the laws concerning the author of dispensations showed some development, not with regard to the general rule that inferiors could not relax a superior's law—which has continued in force without interruption—but with respect to the exception which was made for urgent cases. Nevertheless, it will be seen immediately that this development, if strictly considered, was concerned with a particular kind of dispensation, rather than with dispensations in general.

[9] V. g., Pirhing, *Jus Canonicum,* lib. V. tit. 33, sec. 1, n. 5.

[10] Reiffenstuel, *Jus Canonicum,* lib. I, tit. 3, *de rescriptis,* n. 30: "... Huc reducuntur gratiae illae, quae proprie ac stricte privilegia non sunt, conceduntur tamen contra jus commune: ut sunt dispensationes ... eo quod non concedantur per modum legis privatae, ad operandum ordinarie ac stabiliter contra Jus commune." Schmalzgrueber, *Jus Ecclesiasticum Universum,* lib. V. tit. XXXIII, n. 5.

Several declarations of the Holy See [11] seemed to militate against the above-mentioned opinion of the Decretalists that bishops could relax the Church's laws in cases of "urgent necessity and evident utility of the Church." But they did not explicitly condemn it, and since they were general in character, it appears that they were concerned only with what was the usual case, and not with the exceptional emergency. Moreover, it has been the common opinion of canonists since the age of the later Decretalists that, by way of exception, when an urgent necessity arises requiring a dispensation, the power to dispense is presumed to be communicated to the bishop if it is difficult for him to have recourse to the Holy See and there is danger in delay.[12]

However, as far as matrimonial dispensations were concerned, this opinion later lost its force by reason of several decisions which were reported in an Instruction of the Holy Office, published June 8, 1756.[13] First, there was the *negative* reply, March 13, 1660, to the question of whether "a bishop, in a case of very urgent necessity, can dispense from a public impediment *ante contractum matrimonium.*" Then on January 19, 1661, the Congregation of the Council approved and confirmed the judgment of the theological censors of the Congregation of the Inquisition who branded as "false, rash, scandalous, harmful and seditious the proposition which asserts that a bishop can dispense from the public diriment matrimonial impediment of

[11] S.C.C., *Reatina,* 3 iun. 1592, ad 4: " . . . non licuisse Episcópo dispensare adversus Pontificiam constitutionem, nisi id ei constitutione ipsa expressim permitteretur."—*Fontes,* n. 2244; Clemens VIII, decr. *Nullus omnino,* 25 iul. 1599, § 8: "Superioribus autem, nec Concilii Tridentini, aut hacc nostra decreta declarare, interpretari, aut relaxare ullo modo possint, omnino interdicimus et prohibemus. . ."—*Fontes,* n. 187; S.C.S. Off., instr., 8 iun. 1756—*Collect. S. C. de Prop. Fide,* n. 399.

[12] Suarez, *De legibus,* VI, c. 14, n. 10; Sanchez, *De Matrimonio,* lib. II, disp. 40, n. 3; Reiffenstuel, *Jus Canonicum,* lib. I, tit. 2, n. 470; Ojetti, *Synopsis Rerum Moralium et Juris Pontificii,* p. 147; Zittelli, *Apparatus Iuris Ecclesiastici,* p. 37; Sanguinetti *Iuris Ecclesiastici Privati Institutiones,* p. 53.

[13] *Collect. S. C. de Prop. Fide,* n. 399.

consanguinity for a marriage to be contracted, whether *in articulo mortis,* or in another very urgent necessity in which the contracting parties cannot await the dispensation of the Apostolic See." The Instruction of the Holy Office went on to say; "Wherefore, only a faculty of the Apostolic See or . . . an immemorial, or at least centenary, custom, whence the benign consent of the Roman Pontiff could legitimately be discerned, can render valid a dispensation from public diriment impediments."

This apparent severity was somewhat relaxed later, when under the pontificate of Leo XIII the Holy Office issued an Encyclical Letter [14] in which it was stated that Leo XIII had approved the concession whereby "local Ordinaries can dispense . . . those who are in very grave danger of death, when there is not time to recur to the Holy See, from public diriment matrimonial impediments of ecclesiastical law, except the sacred Order of Priesthood and affinity in the direct line which has arisen from lawful (i.e., in a lawful marriage) intercourse." From the remarks which prefaced the bestowal of this power, as also from a later reply of the Holy Office,[15] it is evident that the concession was limited to cases in which the parties "had civilly married or had been otherwise living in concubinage."

Finally, another reply of the Holy Office [16] confirmed the opinion that the words *super impedimentis quantumvis publicis* used in its Letter of February 20, 1880, signified that *in articulo mortis* local ordinaries can *a fortiori* dispense from occult impediments.

Article IV. Cause

It has been shown that there existed among the Decretists and Decretalists an almost universal agreement that causes of a private nature sufficed for the granting of a dispensation if they were just and reasonable. That this doctrine has continued to be accepted by the Holy See down to the present time is evident from documents which have emanated from the Roman Curia

[14] Feb. 20, 1888—*Collect. S. C. de Prop. Fide,* n. 1685.
[15] Sept. 17, 1890—*Collect. S. C. de Prop. Fide,* n. 1741.
[16] Apr. 23, 1890—*Collect. S. C. de Prop, Fide,* n. 1728.

itself, and which make no reference to the necessity of a public cause, such as the decree of the Congregation for the Propagation of the Faith,[17] which directed that bishops should not grant dispensations "unless an urgent and just reason, or a greater utility, warrant it", the resolution of the Congregation of the Council, which declared that "a dispensation is usually not granted except for a just and reasonable cause," [18] and a later resolution of the same Congregation concerning the dispensation from an impediment (of age) to the obtaining of a canonry, which repeats almost verbatim the preceding Resolution.[19]

This statement is not to be understood to mean that in every case the Holy See would recognize the sufficiency of a private cause. On the contrary, the Church has at times indicated the requirement of a cause of common necessity or utility when certain dispensations were concerned. Thus the Congregation of the Council, with reference to a priest who had become irregular through the loss of his hand, declared that for a dispensation from this irregularity "canonical causes, which are necessity and evident utility of the Church, are required." [20] Such a declaration is, however, exceptional in the sense that it is of rare occurrence. But it cannot be regarded as a real exception to the rule, because the rule has been that a "just and reasonable cause be present." It is merely an evidence that in these instances the Church's requirements of justice and reasonableness are fulfilled only by a cause which implies a common advantage. This, in turn, is a consequence of the special nature of the law in question.[21]

The requirement of the necessity or the evident utility of the Church was apparently set aside later, at least with regard to dispensations from the irregularity mentioned above. For in a similar case a dispensation was granted on the strength

[17] Apr. 13, 1807—*Collect. S. C. de Prop. Fide*, n. 692, ad IX.

[18] Jan. 23, 1847—*Thesaurus Resolutionum S. C. C.*, CVII, 55.

[19] S. C. C., June 20, 1878—*ASS.*, XII (1879), 65-70.

[20] S. C. C., Feb. 24, 1872—*ASS.*, VII (1872), 277-280.

[21] S. C. C., Sept. 9, 1882—*ASS.*, XV (1882), 452-455, with respect to dispensations from an irregularity arising out of illegitimacy.

of causes which were of a private nature—the desire of offering the divine sacrifice and of avoiding the loss consequent upon the failure to discharge the duties which the petitioner's prebend placed upon him.[22]

Moreover, the Holy See has at times indicated that one or the other individual cause—at least alone—would not fulfill the requirements of justice and reasonableness, even though at the same time a public cause was not demanded for the granting of the dispensation in question. Thus, the mere offering of an alms to the poor or to the Church was declared insufficient for the granting of a matrimonial dispensation.[23] Likewise, the alleviation of a priest's poverty was regarded as insufficient to warrant a dispensation from the irregularity of physical defect.[24] Yet, in the case of a dispensation from the obligation of performing the works enjoined by the will of the founder of a benefice, absolute or at least relative poverty was recognized as a sufficient cause.[25]

It would be difficult, if not impossible, to compile an all inclusive list of causes which the Holy See has regarded as fundamentally fulfilling the requirements of justice and reasonableness. Even in the seventeenth century the practical impossibility of drawing up a list of this kind was realized by Pyrrhus, who, while expressly admitting this, nevertheless attempted to enumerate those which were most commonly accepted in the practice of the Holy See.[26] Shortly thereafter, Pax Jordanus incorporated the

[22] S. C. C., Dec. 17, 1881—*ASS.*, XV (1882), 195-196.

[23] S. C. de Prop. Fide, Mar. 11, 1848—*Collect S. C. de Prop. Fide*, n. 1027.

[24] S. C. C., Feb. 24, 1872—*ASS.*, VII (1872), 277-280.

[25] S. C. C., Jan. 23, 1847—*Thesaurus Resolutionum S. C. C.*, CVII, 55.

[26] Pyrrhus, *Praxis Dispensationum*, lib. I, c. I, n. 11: ". . . videndum erit, quaenam sint justae causae de stylo Romanae Curiae receptae et ad praxim deductae; quibus summus Pontifex frequenter, et in dies uti consuevit; nam licet eae quamplurimae sint, quae non ita facile numerari possent . . . nihilominus, quae in ipsa notoria praxi receptae sunt, enumerantur . . . personae merita . . . necessitatis . . . loci . . . temporis . . . utilitas Ecclesiae . . . aetatis . . . scandalum . . . majus bonum . . . futurum bonum . . . eventus rei . . . discretio . . . pietas . . . misericordia . . religio. . ."

same list in his own writings, and added that the granting of a dispensation was, so to speak, necessary (*debita*) as often as these causes were present.[27] Later, these words of Jordanus together with the same list of causes were embodied in a resolution of the Congregation of the Council,[28] which apparently indicated that the Holy See was proposing this as its own doctrine.

In connection with the question of matrimonial dispensations, several noteworthy *demonstrative* lists have been published at various times by the Roman Curia. The first of these was given by the Holy Office, September 26, 1754.[29] A certain Archbishop had proposed to the Congregation several questions relative to the faculty which he had received, namely, to dispense "the poor from the third and fourth simple degrees of consanguinity or affinity." In its reply the Holy Office mentioned nine causes "on account of which a dispensation of this kind *in forma pauperum* is granted by the Apostolic See." They were: 1) previous carnal intercourse between the affianced parties, 2) infamy occasioned by false suspicions concerning the blameless but familiar relations between the parties, 3) super-marriageable age of the woman, 4) the woman's limited prospects of marriage, 5) her lack or insufficiency of dowry, 6) the allaying of hatreds between the nupturients' families, 7) the confirmation of newly established peace between these families, 8) the settling of litigations between the same families, 9) the seriously cherished desire to avoid marriage with heretics, as long as the nupturients give proof of leading a genuine Catholic life.

Another enumeration—the one most commonly referred to—was made by the Congregation for the Propagation of the Faith in its instruction of May 9, 1877.[30] After stating that in general the gravity of the cause must be in accordance with the gravity of the impediment which obstructs the celebration of the marriage, the Congregation, considering it "opportune . . . to enumerate briefly the principal causes, which are usually re-

[27] Pax Jordanus, *Elucubrationes Diversae,* lib. IX, tit. I, n. 9.

[28] July 16, 1836—*Thesaurus Resolutionum S. C. C.,* XCVI, 358-359.

[29] S. C. S. Off.—*Collect. S. C. de Prop. Fide,* n. 393.

[30] *Collect. S. C. de Prop. Fide,* n. 1470.

garded as sufficient for obtaining matrimonial dispensations according to the canonical sanctions and prudent judgment of ecclesiastical provision," proposed a list of sixteen such causes. It comprised the following: 1) the woman's limited prospects of marriage (*angustia loci*), 2) her super-marriageable age (*aetas superadulta*), 3) her lack or insufficiency of dowry, 4) the issue of legal litigation, 5) the poverty of a widow burdened with the care of many children, 6) the advantage and benefit of a peace to be either restored or maintained, 7) excessive, suspected and dangerous familiarity, 8) previous sexual intercourse between the parties, 9) the evil repute of a woman whose familiarity with a relative has given rise to the suspicion of a carnal union between them, 10) the convalidation of an invalid marriage, 11) the danger of a mixed marriage or of the celebration of the marriage before a non-Catholic minister, 12) the danger of incestuous concubinage, 13) the danger of a civil marriage, 14) the removal of grave scandals, 15) the cessation of notorious concubinage, 16) the oustanding merits of one or the other party.

Finally, at the beginning of the present century the Apostolic Datary published a longer list containing twenty-eight such causes.[31] For the most part this enumeration is merely a repetition of the earlier list furnished by the Congregation for the Propagation of the Faith; and although numerically the later list contains twelve additional causes, in several instances two, three, or even four of the Datary's more detailed causes can be considered as included in a single cause of the earlier list.[32] An example of such inclusion is the first cause mentioned in the earlier list, namely, the woman's limited prospects of marriage (*angustia loci*). This cause could well provide for four conditions considered separately by the Datary, namely, 1) the woman's limited prospects of marriage in a single locality, 2) a similar lack of prospects in a number of localities, 3) lack of

[31] *ASS*, XXXIV (1901-1902), 34-35.

[32] For a comparison of the two lists, cf. O'Mara, *Canonical Causes for Matrimonial Dispensations* (The Catholic University of America, Canon Law Studies, n. 96, Washington: The Catholic University of America, 1935), pp. 131-138.

prospects together with insufficiency of dowry outside of the present locality of the woman, 4) the difficulty experienced by a man in reaching the locality with a view to contracting marriage with one of the inhabitants there. There are, however, six causes stated in the Datary's enumeration which are apparently distinct from any and all of the causes contained in the earlier list. These six causes are: 1) the well founded hope for the conversion of the non-Catholic party, 2) the retention of property or of temporal goods within a given family, 3) the perpetuation of the lineage of an illustrious family or provision for the constitution of a royal heir by succession of descent, 4) the maintenance and safeguarding of a family's ancestral honors, 5) the presence of certain reasonable causes, 6) special reasons affecting the petitioners concerning which the Holy See has definite knowledge.

By way of summary it can be said that since the time of the Decretists and Decretalists the Church has required causes which imply a common advantage only if the law from which the dispensation was sought was one which was more closely bound up with the common good. In other words, as a general rule, when the individual case was examined and it was found that justice and reasonableness could be satisfied and that the common good and ecclesiastical discipline would not suffer detriment from the relaxation of the law in question, it was the mind of the Church to regard as sufficient the cause arising out of the special circumstances of the case, whether it was of a private or of a public nature, and whether it was contained in or omitted from the lists of illustrative causes drawn up at various times.

Article V. Interpretation

The doctrine concerning the interpretation of dispensations, as it existed during the period now under consideration, shows that no substantial development occurred in this regard. On the contrary, official declarations, as well as the statements of canonists of the period, merely repeated what had been taught on this question during the preceding period. In other words, the doctrine consisted of a repetition of the general principle that dispensations must be interpreted strictly, since they are odious departures from the common law,[33] together with a repetition of the more detailed statements that, in accordance with this principle, a dispensation can not be interpreted as extending to cases other than those expressly mentioned,[34] nor to persons other than those expressly named.[35]

But, while nothing substantially new was added with respect to the interpretation of dispensations themselves, the canonists added a consideration which had apparently been disregarded in the preceding period, namely, the consideration of the interpretation of the faculty to dispense. In this regard, they maintained that if the faculty were granted in a general way, it could be considered as a favorable concession, and, hence, could receive a broad interpretation.[36] On the contrary, if the faculty were granted for a specified case or for designated cases, it could not be regarded as a grant in favor of the recipient. Consequently, it had to be interpreted strictly.[37]

Article VI. Cessation

A merely cursory consideration of the causes effecting the termination of dispensations, as they were proposed during this period, might lead one to the conclusion that the only difference between the doctrine of this later period and the doctrine of the preceding period was the addition of a third cause of cessation—renunciation by the recipient of a dispensation—to the two previously advanced by the Decretists and the Decretalists, namely, revocation and the cessation of the final cause on

[33] S. C. C. Resolutio *Missae pro populo,* Mar. 28, 1801, *Thesaurus Resolutionum S. C. C.,* LXVII, 87. Cf. also S. C. C., Resolutio *Alatrina,* Aug. 26, 1820, *Thesaurus Resolutionum S. C. C.,* LXXX, 262.

[34] S. C. C., Resolutio *Placentina executionis,* Jan. 31, 1824, cited by Pallottini, *Collectio Resolutionum S. C. C.,* VII, 243 ad 4.

[35] S. C. C., Resolutio *Missae pro populo,* Mar. 28, 1801, *Thesaurus Resolutionum S. C. C.,* LXVII, 87.

[36] De Justis, *De Dispensationibus Matrimonialibus,* lib. I, cap. II, n. 1; Reiffenstuel, *Jus Canonicum Universum,* lib. I, tit. II, par. XVIII, *de dispensatione,* n. 451.

[37] Pyrrhus, *Praxis Dispensationum,* lib. I, cap. V, n. 27.

account of which the dispensation had been granted. Actually, however, there was a notable difference of doctrine on this point in the two periods. For, although with regard to revocation and to the cessation of the final cause, the principles were identical in both periods—namely, that dispensations were terminated by revocation and by the complete cessation of the final cause—they conveyed a different meaning in each of the two periods.

In the first place, an act whereby a dispensation was revoked had been reserved, in the preceding period, to the superior or the successor of the one who had granted the dispensation, unless the dispensation had been granted unlawfully—in which case the grantor also could revoke it. During the later period, there was a different concept of the grantor's revocatory power. If the legislator himself had granted the dispensation his power validly to revoke the same was recognized even in the absence of a just cause for so doing,[38] but the lawfulness of such a revocation depended upon the presence of a just cause.[39] In cases in which the grantor had dispensed by reason of vicarious power —whether ordinary or delegated *ad universalitatem causarum*—his power to recall the dispensation was regarded as dependent upon the presence of a just cause, not only for the lawfulness of his revocation, but also for the validity of it.[40] Finally, if the grantor had been delegated merely for a particular case, he was considered to be devoid of all power to revoke the dispensation, even if there should be a just cause for doing so, since his jurisdiction had been limited to the performance of the one act of granting the dispensation.[41]

Secondly, as already indicated, the principle that the cessation of the final cause would effect the cessation of a dispensation was understood by the Decretists and the Decretalists to mean not that dispensations already granted would cease, but that after the final cause had ceased similar dispensations should not

[38] Suarez, *De legibus,* VI, c. 20, n. 6.

[39] Wernz, *Jus Decretalium,* I, n. 126.

[40] Wernz, *Jus Decretalium,* I, n. 126; Ojetti, *Synopsis Rerum Moralium et Juris Pontificii,* p. 148.

[41] Ojetti, *Synopsis,* p. 148; Wernz, *Jus Decretalium,* I, n. 126.

be granted. In the following period, this principle was applied to dispensations themselves. It was not, however, applied to all dispensations, but only to those which had a successive recurrence.[42]

To these two causes of cessation, there was added, in this later period, the above mentioned third mode of termination, namely, the renunciation of a dispensation by its recipient. Since a dispensation was regarded as a private favor granted to the one who received it, he was free either to use it or not to use it, and, hence, to renounce it if he should so choose.[43] In order, however, that the renunciation of a dispensation might effect, with regard to the dispensed person, the restoration of the law which had been relaxed, it was considered as necessary that the renunciation should be accepted by the competent superior, unless the law in question were one the obliging force of which depended on the free will of the recipient of the dispensation, as in the case of vows.[44]

Finally in connection with this question of renunciation, canonists concluded that the non-use or a contrary usage did not constitute an implicit renunciation of a dispensation.[45]

[42] Suarez, *De legibus,* VI, c. 20, n. 12; Ojetti, *Synopsis,* p. 148.

[43] Suarez, *De legibus,* VI, c. 20, n. 7.

[44] Ojetti, *Synopsis,* p. 148; Wernz, *Jus Decretalium,* I, n. 126.

[45] Suarez, *De legibus,* VI, c. 20, nn. 8, 9; Wernz, *Jus Decretalium,* I, n. 126.

PART II
CANONICAL COMMENTARY

CHAPTER VI

THE ACTIVE SUBJECT OF DISPENSATORY POWER

Article I. Power Exercised in One's Own Right

Canon 80. Dispensatio . . . concedi potest a conditore legis, ab eius successore vel Superiore . . .

The words of canon 80, quoted immediately above, constitute an all-exclusive designation of those who *in their own right* are empowered to grant a dispensation. It is a designation which obtains its force not merely from the fact that it is a disposition of positive law. In reality, it is an expression of an underlying principle, based on the very nature of a dispensation, the granting of which, it will be remembered, implies an act of jurisdiction; a principle which is sufficiently general in character to be applicable to any dispensation, whether it be from the general law of the Church or from some particular law.

In the first place, it is evident that a legislator has power to relax his own law, since the law derives its binding force only from the will of the legislator.[1] For just as the legislator might, at the time when he enacts a law, exempt certain persons from the obligation of his law, so he can, at a later date, will that the obligation of his law should cease as far as the designated individuals are concerned. This is merely an application of the legal maxim which says that "everything can be dissolved by the same causes which brought it into being."[2] When a law constitutes the matter under consideration, the will of the legislator is the cause which produces it.

This dispensatory prerogative of the legislator is, however, official rather than personal, since ordinary jurisdiction is at-

[1] Suarez, *De legibus,* VI, c. 14, n. 2.
[2] C. 1, X, *de regulis iuris,* V, 41.

tached to an office and the legislator personally participates in it only because he occupies that office. Any law which he establishes is a product of his will *as an official,* which is formally distinct from his will as a human being. In like manner a dispensation is an act of his official will. Accordingly, if for any cause he has ceased to occupy the office by reason of which he was in possession of jurisdictional powers, his right to dispense has simultaneously ceased. For example, a bishop who has resigned his diocese because of ill health cannot grant a dispensation from a law which he established as ordinary of that diocese.

Secondly, a successor can dispense his predecessor's law because officially he is identical with his predecessor. He has the same jurisdiction, since he occupies the same office, and according to another legal maxim "he who succeeds to the right of another must use the same right."[3]

Thirdly, one who is jurisdictionally superior to a legislator can relax the laws of that legislator because the inferior's jurisdiction is dependent upon the superior's.[4] Moreover, to deny this right to a superior would be equivalent to admitting that an inferior has the right to impede the will of the superior—a claim which surely cannot be maintained.

COMPETENCE OF THE VARIOUS ECCLESIASTICAL SUPERIORS

A. Roman Pontiff

Canon 81. A generalibus Ecclesiae legibus Ordinarii infra Romanum Pontificem dispensare nequeunt. . .

The Code does not contain an explicit declaration of the extent of the Pope's dispensatory power, but from the principle enunciated in canon 80, together with the implication contained in canon 81, one can deduce that the dispensatory power of the Roman Pontiff includes within its scope any purely ecclesiastical law, whether it has been enacted by himself, by one of his

[3] Reg. 46, R. J. in VI°.

[4] Suarez, *De legibus,* VI, c. 14, n. 2.

predecessors, by the Apostles, by an ecumenical council, or, finally, by a legislator who exercises jurisdiction only over some particular territory or particular society. In these cases the Roman Pontiff is jurisdictionally either equal or superior to the legislator.[5] In this connection it is especially imperative to remember that the principle expressed in canon 80 is more fundamental than any rule of mere positive law. In other words it is not merely from Canon Law that the Pope derives this power.

The truth of this universal papal dispensatory power is but a corollary of the doctrine which proclaims the plenitude of jurisdiction enjoyed by the Roman Pontiff. The Vatican Council[6] declared that the Pope "has . . . supreme and full power of jurisdiction in the universal Church . . . over those things which pertain to the discipline and government of the Church throughout the whole world." Accordingly, all merely ecclesiastical laws are subject to his power in such a way that he can dispense from any one of them at any time. If, however, a dispensation from such an ecclesiastical law, by reason of particular attendant circumstances, entailed also a violation of the divine law, the Roman Pontiff would not be empowered to grant the dispensation. Thus, if the granting of a dispensation would constitute an injustice to a third party, then the Pope could not grant it. The divine law would naturally prevail. This has been the common teaching of authors,[7] and it has been substantiated by the practice and decrees of the Holy See.[8]

[5] Suarez, *De legibus,* VI, c. 14, n. 2.

[6] Sess. IV, cap. 3 [De primatu Romani Pontificis]—Denzinger-Bannwart, *Enchiridion Symbolorum* (10 ed., Friburgi Brisgoviae: Herder, 1908), n. 1831.

[7] The principle establishing the Pope's universal power has, at times, received a more limited application due to the different concept of what precisely was included under the term "ecclesiastical law," but the principle itself was accepted. Cf. Suarez, *De legibus,* VI, c. 14, n. 2; Reiffenstuel, *Jus Canonicum Universum,* lib. I, tit. 2, n. 455 sq.; St. Thomas, *Quodlibetum,* IV, a. 13; Michiels, *Normae Generales,* II, 478.

[8] Cf. the numerous citations in the footnotes to canon 218, which canon is a brief restatement of the Vatican Council's delaration. Cf. also the condemnation by Sixtus IV of the proposition: "Papa non potest

Moreover, the faculty to relax, *by proper power,* a general law of the Church resides in the Roman Pontiff alone, exclusive of all others who enjoy some measure of ecclesiastical jurisdiction. It might be said, in theory, that an ecumenical council enjoys the same right with reference to laws enacted by itself or by a former council, but in practice a council never grants a dispensation.

Reason alone is sufficient to confirm the exclusiveness of this papal prerogative. For the same power is necessary to relax a law as was required to enact it; and where there is a question of a general law of the Church this power is clearly lacking in any authority below that of the Pope.[9] Suarez [10] expresses the same idea when he says: "An inferior can not annul or impede the will of a superior, not only in the presence of the latter's positive unwillingness, but also in the absence of his actual consent; therefore, he can not dispense from the superior's law merely because a special prohibition is lacking but there is required a positive concession made through an express willingness of the superior or at least through a tacit willingness made known in some sufficient manner. The first part [i.e., that the non-existence of a special prohibition is insufficient] is clear . . . because an inferior power cannot impede a superior power and . . . because correct government demands that the superior's will should prevail over that of an inferior, unless the superior permits otherwise. In order that this might be effected it is necessary that he [the superior] remove his former will—a thing which is brought about only through a positive consent or concession. The second part [i.e., that a positive concession is necessary] is evident because a dispensation takes away the will of the superior, or impedes its effect in a particular matter. . . "

To these arguments derived from reason and from the nature

dispensare in statutis universalis Ecclesiae"—Denzinger-Bannwart, *Enchiridion Symbolorum,* n. 731.

[9] Brys, "De potestate Episcoporum dispensandi in legibus Ecclesiae generalibus," *Collationes Brugenses,* XXIX (1929), 144.

[10] *De legibus,* VI, c. 14, n. 4.

of the power of jurisdiction can be added the positive disposition of canon 81, namely, that "ordinaries other than the Roman Pontiff can not grant a dispensation from the general laws of the Church, not even in a particular case. . . . "[11] By this declaration, as far as the general laws of the Church are concerned, the power enjoyed by ordinaries other than the Roman Pontiff is limited to participated or derived power.

B. Other Ordinaries

Canon 82. Episcopi aliique locorum Ordinarii dispensare valent in legibus dioecesanis . . . non vero in legibus quas speciatim tulerit Romanus Pontifex pro illo peculiari territorio, nisi ad normam can. 81.

Another immediate deduction to be drawn from the principle expressed in canon 80 is that a local ordinary[12] is endowed with proper power within the limits of his own territory to relax a law established either by himself or by one of his predecessors, even if such a law was enacted in a synod, for the reason that "in a synod there is only one legislator namely, the bishop." The others who are present have only a consultive vote.[13] Nor need

[11] This is a substantial restatement of the principle enunciated by Clement V (1305-1314): "The law of a superior cannot be removed by his inferior"—C. 2, *Ne Romani,* I, 3, in Clem.

[12] Included under the term "local ordinary" are the following: 1. Residential bishops, 2. Abbots and Prelates *Nullius,* 3. vicars-general of the foregoing, 4. Apostolic Administrators, 5. vicars and prefects apostolic, 6. superiors of missions *sui iuris,* 7. *vicarii delegati* of vicars and prefects apostolic and of the superiors of missions *sui iuris,* 8. those who, from the prescriptions of law or approved custom, succeed to those mentioned above, that is: a) the chapter (of the cathedral or of the abbey or prelacy *nullius)* until the election of a capitular vicar, b) the capitular vicar—in territories where a chapter is not established, the diocesan consultors and, in turn, the elected administrator take the places of the chapter and the capitular vicar respectively, c) the pro-vicar, d) the pro-prefect, e) the pro-superior. Cf. canons 198, §§ 1, 2; 312; 319; 327; 309; 431; 432; S. C. de Prop. Fide, Dec. 8, 1919—*AAS.,* XII (1920), 120; Pugliese, "De Vicario Delegato in territorio missionum," *Apollinaris,* VI (1933), 196-217.

[13] Can. 362.

the local ordinary seek the consent or the counsel of his cathedral chapter—the diocesan consultors, in places where no cathedral chapter has been established — in order to grant a dispensation from a law of this kind, even though the chapter had been asked to give its assent to the enactment of the law, and had actually consented.[14]

The proper authority of local ordinaries, however, does not extend to laws which the Roman Pontiff has established for a particular territory.[15] For, while a law of this kind is strictly a particular law, it is none the less an enactment of an authority superior to the local ordinary; and an inferior possesses no proper authority over the laws of a superior.[16]

Prior to the Code the competence of ordinaries over such laws was disputed. Some authors [17] maintained that these laws, inasmuch as they are particular laws, fall within the scope of the ordinary's jurisdiction, while others more correctly denied the ordinary's power—unless the law was one of frequent occurrence or unless a custom substantiated his claim—if without grave inconvenience the dispensation could be sought from the Roman Pontiff.[18]

Canon 82 uses the phrase *Episcopi aliique locorum Ordinarii,* but this should not be interpreted to mean that all bishops obtain the dispensatory power referred to by the very fact that they are bishops. The sense of it is rather that bishops who are local ordinaries (i.e., residential bishops) as well as other local ordinaries have this power. In other words, titular bishops who possess only the power of orders do not receive from this canon the power which belongs to local ordinaries. This is merely a deduction from the very fundamental principle that dispensations can be granted only by one who is in possession of adequate *juris diction.*

With respect to the power exercised by vicars general of resi-

[14] Benedictus XIV, *De Synodo Dioecesana,* lib. XIII, c. 5, n. 7.
[15] Can. 82.
[16] Wernz, *Ius Decretalium,* I, 140.
[17] V. g., Cajetanus, cited by Suarez, *De legibus,* VI, c. 14, n. 10.
[18] Suarez, *De legibus,* VI, c. 14, n. 10.

dential bishops and of abbots and prelates *nullius,* it must be admitted that they enjoy the right to relax laws enacted by the principal ordinary or his predecessor. They are themselves local ordinaries [19] and consequently are included under the terms of canon 82. But, because the jurisdiction which they exercise is only vicarious, and accordingly particpiated, any dispensation which they grant is given not on their own proper authority, but in the name of the local ordinary whose vicars they are. This also applies to the *vicarius delegatus* in mission territories.

Major Superiors of exempt clerical institutes [20] can, in virtue of their own authority, dispense their subjects from a law which they themselves have established or which one of their predecessors or inferiors has enacted. To this general rule an exception is to be made with respect to the Abbot Primate and the superior of a monastic congregation. Although they are major superiors, they do not receive the same unqualified jurisdiction which the common law gives to other major superiors. They possess only such "power and jurisdicition as is granted to them either by the constitutions of their own institute or by special decrees of the Holy See." [21] Accordingly, if their constitutions are silent on the question of their dispensatory power, these two classes of superiors must be considered as devoid of proper power to dispense.

Article II. Derived Dispensatory Power

Canon 80. Dispensatio . . . concedi potest . . . nec non ab illo cui iidem (conditor legis, eius successor vel Superior) facultatem dispensandi concesserint.

A person who has the right to do something possesses fundamentally the corresponding right to commission someone else to perform that act in his stead.[22] Since this is true, it follows that the legislator, his successor or his superior can empower another

[19] Can. 198, § 2.
[20] Can. 488, 8º.
[21] Can. 501, § 3.
[22] Reg. 68, R. J. in VIº.

person to grant dispensations from any laws enacted by that legislator. Such a concession of power can be made, however, only to a cleric, because clerics alone are capable of obtaining the power of jurisdiction.[23]

At first glance, it would appear from canon 80 that one who receives such a commission receives from the legislator (or his successor or superior) only *delegated* power to dispense, because the words seem to indicate a special personal concession on the legislator's part made to another designated individual. While this is often the case, it is not always so. At times the legislator makes a concession of dispensatory power in the law itself. At such times, if the faculty is bestowed directly on a certain office and indirectly on the incumbent because he is actually occupying that office, the jurisdiction which the commissioned person enjoys is not delegated but ordinary power.[24] In a number of places the Code grants this kind of power, for example, when it states that ordinaries can relax the general laws of the Church if the extraordinary circumstances are present which are mentioned in the last part of canon 81.

There are some authors [25] who maintain that the power to relax a superior's law which ordinaries receive from the law itself is always delegated, and never ordinary. They contend that for ordinary power something more is required than the concession of a faculty to an office. In their opinion the power must be "proper to the office, that is, it must belong to the office *per se* (and not only through a commission) according to the preformed juridical concept in the constitutional law."

In support of the opposite opinion, however, it can be said that canon 197 is verbatim a restatement of the old law, namely, "ordinary power of jurisdiction is that which is attributed by the law itself to an office." Under the old law the power which ordinaries possessed because of such a commission was commonly

[23] Can. 118.

[24] Can. 197.

[25] V.g., Ojetti, *Commentarium in Codicem Iuris Canonici,* (Romae: apud aedes Universitatis Gregorianae, 1927), I, 328, nota 10.

interpreted as being ordinary; and by reason of canon 6, n. 2, that is likewise the way it is to be understood under the law of the Code. Furthermore, canon 912 can be advanced against Ojetti's concept of ordinary power. For, while this canon does not refer to the relaxation of a law, it gives evident proof that inferiors can obtain ordinary jurisdiction over matters which pertain *per se* to a superior authority. The canon states: "Besides the Roman Pontiff to whom the administration of the entire spiritual treasury of the Church has been entrusted by Christ the Lord, they alone can grant indulgences by ordinary power to whom this is expressly granted by law." [26]

COMPETENCE OF THE VARIOUS ECCLESIASTICAL SUPERIORS

A. Roman Pontiff

It is customary for canonists to include in their treatises on dispensation a statement of the Roman Pontiff's [27] ordinary vicarious power to "dispense" for a just cause from precepts of the divine law, the obliging force of which depends on the former consent of the human will, as in the case of vows, oaths, or ratified non-consummated marriages. They include it because of the similarity of the effect of such a dispensation, although with very few exceptions [28] they agree that the exercise of this

[26] Cf. Michiels, *Normae Generales*, II, 469-471; Generosus Crisci, "Evolutio historica delegationis a iure," *Apollinaris*, IX (1936), 270-299; "De delegatione a iure in iure canonico vigenti," *Apollinaris*, X (1937), 513-535; Cappello, *Summa*, I, n. 130; De Meester, *Iuris Canonici Compendium*, (nova ed. Brugis: Societas Sancti Augustini, 1921), I, nn. 444-448; A Coronata, *Institutiones*, I, n. 278, nota 3; Vermeersch-Creusen, *Epitome Iuris Canonici* (3 ed. Mechliniae-Romae: Dessain, 1927), I, n. 277; Engel, *Collegium Universi Iuris Canonici*, lib. I, tit. 29, n. 4.

[27] To a certain extent, local ordinaries and religious superiors likewise participate in this power through the Roman Pontiff. Cf. can. 1313. Cf. also Wernz, *Ius Decretalium*, III, 602.

[28] A Coronata, *Institutiones Iuris Canonici*, I, 106, nota 3: ". . .Alii vero explicant facilius rem, dicendo veram potestatem dispensandi in his concessam esse a Christo; Codex cum in his casibus loquatur de dispensatione, et quidem ut distinguitur ab irritatione (cc. 1311, 1312, 1313, 1320, etc., una cum c. 18), huic alteri opinioni calculum adiecisse videtur."

power does not constitute a true dispensation, that is a direct and absolute removal of the obligation of the divine law. Rather, the Pope's power operates directly on the act of the human will as such, remitting in the name of God the obligation or bond (arising out of that human act) by nullifying the operative effect of the human act whence the obligation or bond arises. As a consequence of this remission, the obligation of the divine law, whether positive or natural, ceases to exist.[29]

In order to substantiate the existence of this power over such divine laws it is necessary only to indicate the vicarious power which Christ conferred on Peter and his successors in the words, "Whatsoever thou shalt bind upon earth, it shall be bound also in heaven; and whatsoever thou shalt loose upon earth it shall be loosed also in heaven."[30] For, although there is no explicit mention of this particular power in these words of Christ, it is sufficiently contained therein. Christ's words are so general in character that they include the remission of any bond which is not in itself and absolutely indissoluble, unless, of course, with respect to one or the other bond Christ has withheld the power.[31] A ratified and consummated marriage, for example, is one such case in which the power to "dispense" has been withheld.[32] On the contrary, however, there is no indication that Christ excluded from His broad communication of power the vicarious faculty to remit the natural obligation resulting, for instance, from vows, oaths or unconsummated marriages, even though these should be ratified marriages.

This interpretation of Christ's words has, moreover, been the traditional teaching of the Church from the earliest times, and it

[29] Suarez, *De legibus,* II, c. 14; Schmalzgrueber, *Ius Ecclesiasticum,* lib. I, tit. 2, nn. 56-57; Wernz, *Ius Decretalium,* I, n. 122; Cicognani-O'Hara-Brennan, *Canon Law,* (2 ed., Philadelphia: The Dolphin Press, 1935), pp. 836-837.

[30] Matt. XIV, 19. Cf. also Matt. XVIII, 18.

[31] Suarez, *De Statu Perfectionis et Religionis,* tract. VII, lib. VI, c. 16, n. 11: " . . . ab universali Christi locutione non excipere possumus, nisi quod vel natura sua exceptum est, vel Christus ipse excepit."

[32] Matt. XIX, 4-6; can. 1118.

has been supported by the Church's traditional practice of granting such "dispensations" when a just cause has been present to warrant the exercise of this power. In view of this tradition based on Christ's words it would be, to say the least, rash to assert that the Church had usurped and arrogated to herself so fundamental a power.[33]

B. The Roman Curia

Occupying, as it were, a middle position between the dispensatory power personally possessed by the Roman Pontiff and that of the inferior ordinaries throughout the Church is the power invested in the various dicasteries of the Roman Curia. Since it would be impossible for the Roman Pontiff personally to attend to all of the numerous affairs of the Church, the Sacred Congregations, Tribunals and Offices, each with its respective competence, have been established, and to each the Pope entrusts a share in his jurisdiction in such a way that each is empowered to expedite matters pertinent to its own designated field of activity when these matters are brought to the attention of the Holy See. These dicasteries, as they are called, of the Roman Curia function in the name of the Roman Pontiff, and as a consequence, their authority is quasi-supreme, even though naturally it is lower than the absolutely supreme authority personally invested in the Pope.

The competence of the several dicasteries is, of course, determined by the Roman Pontiff; and although he can certainly enlarge or restrict the power of any one of them at any time, their competence has been established rather precisely in the Code.[34] In matters which are not of an extraordinary nature the dicasteries exercise their dispensatory power in accordance with their competence as thus established by law, together with the

[33] Suarez, *De Voto,* VI, c. 9, n. 18; Wernz, *Ius Decretalium,* III, 602; Teodori, "Consultationes," *Apollinaris,* VI (1933), 370.

[34] Can. 246-264. Cf. also the *motu proprio* of Pius XI, *Sancta Dei Ecclesia,* March 25, 1938—*AAS.,* *XXX* (1938), 154-159, which extended the jurisdiction of the Congregation for the Oriental Church, so that it now embraces those of the Latin rite who live in certain territories.

competence which they receive from special faculties of the Pope. If the matter is one of an extraordinary nature, the dicasteries may not concern themselves with it, unless their respective moderator has first notified the Roman Pontiff; and with respect to dispensations pontifical approval is necessary, unless faculties for granting the dispensation in question have been given to the dicastery which is dealing with the affair.[35]

Restriction of Dicastery's Power by Reason of a Previous Refusal of the Dispensation

A noteworthy restriction of power is contained in canon 43, which declares invalid the granting of a favor by one Sacred Congregation or Office of the Roman Curia if the same favor has previously been refused by another Sacred Congregation or Office. The canon, however, leaves intact the right of the Sacred Penitentiary to grant favors for the internal forum. In view of the fact that one or the other Dicastery is *exclusively* competent for practically every matter which can be presented in the external forum, it is very rarely that a case such as is here considered can arise.[36] When, however, a case does arise in which two Congregations or Offices are competent to grant the requested dispensation, and a request is made to the second dicastery after one of them has refused it, the consent of the first is a necessary condition for the valid relaxation of the law.

Some authors maintain that the same invalidating effect is not produced if a dispensation is granted by one of the Congregations or Offices after it has been refused by the Roman Pontiff. They base their contention on the fact that the law of canon 43 is one which restricts the free exercise of rights and therefore, in accordance with canon 19, it must be interpreted strictly.[37]

[35] Can. 244.

[36] As will be seen later, the same law applies likewise to the granting of favors by local ordinaries. In these circumstances it can more easily arise.

[37] Michiels, *Normae Generales*, II, 178-179; A Coronata, *Institutiones*, I, 62; Cappello, *Summa*, I, n. 145.

While admitting that according to the strict letter of the law canon 43 does not invalidate such a dispensation granted after the Pope's refusal to relax the law, it seems that the invalidity must be admitted for reasons other than the simple prescription of canon 43. In the first place there is no express prescription of law which precisely covers this point. Consequently the provisions of canon 20 must be employed. Among the sources from which, according to canon 20, the norm is to be derived are the "general principles of law observed with canonical equity." It would be unreasonable if a vicar were empowered to impede the will of him whose vicar he is, especially when the superior is the supreme authority. But that is precisely what would result if a Congregation or Office could relax a law after the Pope had expressed his will that the obligation of the law should not be relaxed. His refusal of the request would constitute such an expression of will. Furthermore, there is the legal maxim that "if something is forbidden a person in one way, then another way must not be admitted for gaining it." [38] In fine, although canon 11 provides that "only those laws are to be considered invalidating or disqualifying which expressly or equivalently state that an act is null or a person is incapable of acting," it seems reasonable that, in view of the more basic principles stated immediately above, the denial of a dispensation by the Roman Pontiff should be regarded as an implicit restriction of the dicastery's competence. Any one of the dicasteries must be regarded as the Pope's agent. As such its power depends on the will of the sovereign Pontiff; and it is most improbable that he would will that it should be empowered to grant a dispensation which he himself has refused.

Inasmuch as the restriction of competence, under consideration at present, as well as the similar restriction with reference to local ordinaries, which will be treated later, is included in the Code under the title of "Rescripts," and inasmuch as a rescript is considered as a *written* reply, the question can be raised as to whether the oral refusal of a dispensation will produce the same

[38] Reg. 84, R. J. in VI°.

effect as does a written refusal. For the reasons just stated one could conceive of the possibility of a distinction, but there seems to be no solid basis for saying that the refusal of a dispensation by one Congregation or Office would not invalidate the concession of the same dispensation by another Congregation or Office, merely because the refusal had not been in writing.

Aside from the fact that the method of refusal does not alter the underlying principles which demonstrate the invalidity, a proof can be found in the statements of canons 43 and 44. These canons employ the term *gratia* without adding any qualification. Consequently, what is said must be considered as applying to any favor, since no reason for drawing a distinction is apparent either in the law itself or otherwise from the nature of things. It is only natural that these canons should be included in the title of "Rescripts," because the ordinary means of granting or refusing any favor, dispensations included, is by rescript. An oral concession or refusal is extraordinary; and as a general rule laws are concerned rather with what is ordinary. Furthermore, that the legislator did not intend that canons 43 and 44 should refer only to the so called rescripts of favor is apparent from the fact that elsewhere, for example, in canon 38, he uses the clause *rescripta quibus gratia conceditur,* while in the present canon he avoids this clause and legislates by using the unqualified term *gratia.*

C. Other Ordinaries

Canon 81. A generalibus Ecclesiae legibus Ordinarii infra Romanum Pontificem dispensare nequeunt, ne in casu quidem peculiari, nisi haec potestas eisdem fuerit explicite vel implicite concessa, aut nisi difficilis sit recursus ad Sanctam Sedem et simul in mora sit periculum gravis damni, et de dispensatione agatur quae a Sede Apostolica concedi solet.

Canon 82. Episcopi aliique locorum Ordinarii dispensare valent in legibus dioecesanis, et in legibus Concilii provincialis ac plenarii ad normam can. 291, § 2, non vero in legibus quas speciatim tulerit

Romanus Pontifex pro illo peculiari territorio, nisi ad normam can. 81.

In the historical treatise reference was made to the fact that even among those who were agreed in denying to inferior ordinaries any proper power over the Church's general laws, a divergence of opinion sometimes existed with respect to their derived power of relaxing such laws. There was, for example, the opinion, sustained by some but denied by others, that bishops could relax these laws in the absence of an explicit prohibition to the contrary.[39] Although the legal doctrine concerning ordinaries' power over general laws is included, at least in a negative way, in the principle enunciated in canon 80, the legislator, mindful no doubt of this past difference of opinion, sought to preclude the possibility of any doubt on this score by fixing definitely and explicitly the limits of the ordinaries' power in this regard. The general rule was formulated that "ordinaries . . . even in a particular case cannot dispense from general laws of the Church, unless this power has been granted to them either explicitly or implicitly, or unless recourse to the Holy See is difficult and simultaneously there is danger of grave harm in delay and the dispensation is one which the Holy See is wont to grant."[40]

A "particular case" is one in which a dispensation is granted to particular persons for a just cause.[41] But since a particular case is excluded from the competence of an ordinary, it follows that the granting of a dispensation in a general case—such as the relaxation of a law in favor of all his subjects—is certainly not within the competence of the ordinary.

1. Express Concession

Since canon 81 speaks of ordinaries without qualification, the

[39] *Supra*, p. 30. Cf. also Suarez, De legibus, VI, c. 14, n. 3.

[40] Can. 81.

[41] Van Hove, cited by Brys, " De potestate Episcoporum dispensandi in legibus Ecclesiae generalibus," *Collationes Brugenses*, XXIX (1929), 144; Augustine, *A Commentary on the New Code of Canon Law* (4 ed., St. Louis: B. Herder, 1921), I, 178; Vermeersch-Creusen, *Epitome*, I, n. 174.

faculty to dispense in the given circumstances is enjoyed not only by local ordinaries,[42] but also by major superiors of clerical exempt institutes, with respect to their own subjects.[43]

An *explicit concession* of dispensatory power is made whenever a superior clearly indicates such power either by the express words of a law or special indult, or by means of some other sign which distinctly expresses it.[44]

In order to facilitate the government of the Church at large and the better to provide for the greater good and salvation of the faithful, it has for centuries been the custom of the Holy See to grant ample dispensatory faculties to ordinaries. This power is conferred in various ways.

I. The law itself occasionally grants dispensatory power. Examples of such power found in the Code are the following: a) with respect to all ordinaries indiscriminately, the faculty (1) to dispense when there exists a doubt of fact, if the law is one which the Roman Pontiff is wont to relax (canon 15), (2) to dispense from any law which the Holy See is wont to relax when recourse to the Holy See is difficult and at the same time there is danger of grave harm in delay (canon 81), (3) to dispense from the prescribed observance of holydays and of days of fast or abstinence or of both (canon 1245); b) with respect only to local ordinaries, the faculty (1) to relax in particular cases and for a just cause, the decrees of provincial and plenary councils (canon 291, § 2), (2) to dispense, with the consent of the synodal examiners, a priest from the examination which must otherwise be undergone by a priest who is to be appointed pastor of a parish (canon 459, § 3, 3°), (3) to dispense from the law which stipulates that mixed marriages must be celebrated outside the church building (canon 1109, § 3).[45]

[42] *Supra*, p. 55.

[43] Can. 198, § 1; 488, 2°, 8°.

[44] Brys, "De potestate Episcoporum dispensandi in legibus Ecclesiae generalibus," *Collationes Brugenses*, XXIX (1929), 145; A Coronata, *Institutiones*, I, 107; Michiels, *Normae Generales*, II, 480.

[45] Cf. also, for all ordinaries: canons 972, § 1; 990, § 1; 998, § 1; 1313; 1320; 1444; 2237; for local ordinaries only: 130, § 1; 131, § 3; 1028; 1043; 1045, §§ 1, 2; for religious ordinaries only: 589, § 2; 590.

II. Special concessions of faculties are sometimes made by the Pope personally or by the competent Roman Congregations—again, at times to all ordinaries; at other times, only to local ordinaries. Thus, after the world war the Sacred Consistorial Congregation granted: a) to all ordinaries the faculty to dispense their priests, returning from military service, who were laboring under an irregularity *ex defectu corporis,* when from the written testimony of the master of ceremonies it was clear that these priests could observe all the necessary rites in the celebration of Mass without someone else's assistance, and b) to diocesan ordinaries the five year faculty (1) to place two or even three parishes under the care of one priest, if there was not a sufficient number of priests to assign one to each parish, and also (2) to transfer the pastors from their own parishes to a more central one, in order the better to care for the faithful committed to them.[46]

The quinquennial faculties granted to our bishops constitute another example of such a concession.

A commentary of each individual instance of the Code's concession of dispensatory power is beyond the scope of this dissertation. There is, however, one such example which seems to warrant at least a brief commentary. For, while it can truly be classified as a particular rule, it nevertheless participates to a certain extent in the nature of a general norm.

Canon 15 provides that "in a doubt of fact an ordinary can dispense from all laws provided that the law in question is one from which the Roman Pontiff is wont to grant a dispensation." A doubt of fact exists when it is uncertain whether an act or a person has the conditions required for the application of the law.[47]

Not every doubt of fact, however, will suffice for the employment of this canon. On the contrary, the uncertainty must be positive and must have some objective foundation. A doubt is positive

[46] Decretum S. C. Consist., Oct. 25, 1918—*AAS.*, X (1918), 481-486.

[47] Bouuaert-Simenon, *Manuale Juris Canonici,* (3 ed., Leodii: De Meester, 1930), I, 95; A Coronata, *Institutiones,* I, 18; Cicognani-O'Hara-Brennan, *Canon Law,* p. 585.

when weighty reasons are present both for affirming and for denying the fact. It is negative, if there are present no reasons or only slight reasons for affirming or denying the fact. A doubt has objective foundation if, in the nature of things, there is something which gives rise to the doubt existing in the mind. It is a subjective doubt if there is no such objective foundation for it. A positive doubt is required for the exercise of the power granted in canon 15, because that is the only kind which would remain in the mind of an ordinarily prudent man—who can be taken as a norm—and because a doubt which is merely negative and subjective is equivalent to ignorance, with which the present canon is not concerned.

The concession, however, is not made unless there is question of a law which the Roman Pontiff is accustomed to relax. It would, of course, not be reasonable if an ordinary were to be empowered to grant a dispensation which the Roman Pontiff would not ordinarily grant. For there are certain laws which the Pope does not relax, even though he has the power to do so. In this category the laws, for example, which establish the matrimonial impediments of the sacred order of priesthood, of affinity in the direct line if the valid marriage which has given rise to the affinity has been comsummated and, outside the danger of death, of public and notorious conjugicide.[48]

Whenever, therefore, the conditions of this canon are fulfilled the ordinary need not have recourse to the Holy See, because he himself is empowered to grant the doubtfully required dispensation.

An *implicit concession* of dispensatory power is one which, although not specifically stated, is nevertheless certainly contained in an explicitly given faculty "as an effect in its cause, as a conclusion in a principle, as a species in a genus, as a part in the whole or, in fine, as a condition without which the explicitly granted power cannot be understood or exercised." [49]

[48] Cicognani-O'Hara-Brennan, *Canon Law,* p. 588.

[49] Michiels, *Normae Generales,* II. 481; A Coronata, *Institutiones,* I, 107.

At times the statement of a law makes impersonal mention of the possibility of dispensations from this law by the addition of clauses such as *nisi fuerit misericorditer dispensatum*, or *possit dispensari*.[50] When such a clause is not accompanied by a designation of the one who is empowered to grant the dispensation in question, canonists agree, and have agreed for centuries, that the clause constitutes an implicit concession of power to inferior ordinaries, unless, of course, it is clearly evident that it is not the intention of the legislator to make such a concession.[51] Otherwise, they maintain, these words would be superfluous, since it is not necessary for the legislator to state the obvious truth that he himself has the power to relax his own law.

Likewise, an implicit faculty to dispense from one law contains at times the implicit power to relax another related law, that is, if and when there exists between the two laws an interrelationship which flows *from the very nature* of the two laws and which, as a consequence, will necessitate in every instance the relaxation of the second law if the dispensation of the first law (for which there is an explicitly granted faculty) is to obtain its ultimate effect. Thus the law prescribing residence in a residential benefice[52] is so bound up with the law forbidding the plurality of residential benefices,[53] that in no case could a dispensation from the latter attain its ultimate effect unless the former law were likewise relaxed. Consequently, if an ordinary were granted the explicit faculty to dispense one of his subjects from the law forbidding the plurality of residential benefices, he would also be implicitly authorized to dispense that subject from the law of continually residing in one or the other of these benefices. The Code con-

[50] V.g., c. 12, X, *De poenis*, V, 37; c. 7, X, *De clerico excommunicato*, V, 27.

[51] Suarez, *De legibus*, VI, c. 14. n. 8: Reiffenstuel, *Jus Canonicum Universum*, lib. I, tit. 2, nn. 467-468; A Coronata, *Institutiones*, I, 107, nota 1; Sanchez, *Tractatus de Matrimonio*, lib. VIII, disp. 5, n. 1; Michiels *Normae Generales*, II, 482; Barbosa, *De Officio et Potestate Episcopi*, part. 2, alleg. 33, n. 22.

[52] Can. 1411, 3º.

[53] Can. 1439.

firms this opinion in two places when it says: (1) "Faculties granted by the Holy See include also such powers as are necessary for their exercise . . . ";[54] and (2) " . . . It is understood that a person to whom delegated jurisdiction is given receives also such power as is necessary to make his delegated jurisdiction effective."[55]

The foregoing designation of the circumstances when a concession of such implicit power is present is distinct from that other type of case in which two or more dispensations are required for the ultimate effectiveness of any one of these dispensations, but in which the laws in question are not *naturally* interrelated and consequently are not of necessity present in every instance. Such a case was contemplated under the old law in the instruction of the Holy Office, September 16, 1824.[56] In accordance with the law of the Code, the same congregation rejected the pertinent part of this instruction,[57] namely, that "the Church, when dispensing a Catholic party from the matrimonial impediment of disparity of worship in order that he might contract marriage with an infidel, is understood to dispense also from those impediments from which the infidel is exempt, so that the exemption of the infidel, because of the individual nature of the contract, is communicated to the other [Catholic] party."

Some authors [58] maintain that an implicit concession of power is made "when the Code leaves it to the judgment of the ordinary whether or not a general law is to be observed in a particular case." As examples they give canons 126, 131, 139, 465, 466, 599, 604, 606, 978, § 2. From these instances, however, it seems inaccurate to say that *implicit* dispensatory power is granted. Para-

[54] Can. 66, § 3.

[55] Can. 200, § 1.

[56] *Fontes,* n. 866.

[57] S. C. S. Off., Apr. 15, 1931, cited by Gasparri, *Tractatus Canonicus de Matrimonio* (ed. nova ad mentem Codicis Juris Canonici, Romae: Typis Polyglottis Vaticanis, 1932), I, 367; S. C. de Prop. Fide, May 20, 1931, cited by Bouscaren, *The Canon Law Digest* (Milwaukee: Bruce Publishing Co., 1934), I, 513.

[58] V.g., Bouuaert-Simenon, *Manuale Juris Canonici,* I, n. 230.

graph 3 of canon 131 determines who should attend the conferences prescribed by paragraph 1 of the same canon and it provides that they must be present "unless they have previously obtained an exemption from the local ordinary." This clear statement apparently constitutes an explicit rather than an implicit communication of power. It might be added, in passing, that although this canon uses the word "exemption," it would seem that a true dispensation is meant since the obligation to attend the conference is present unless the local ordinary relaxes the law. In all the other canons cited above as examples of an implicit concession, with the execption of canon 978, § 2, a permission rather than a dispensation is required for the lawful nonobservance of the law in question. Such laws (i. e., requiring permission) do not constitute absolute prohibitions or prescriptions. What is commanded or forbidden is conditioned on the absence of the ordinary's (or superior's) permission to the contrary. If he has granted permission, no dispensation is necessary.[59] Nor is a dispensation necessary in the case of canon 978, § 2. For the obligation of observing the interstices between the reception of the various orders ceases as soon as, in the judgment of the bishop, necessity or the utility of the Church calls for a curtailment of the usual intervals.

Another opinion prevalent among authors prior to the Code maintained that a presumed concession was to be derived from a reasonable interpretation of the legislator's will with reference to matters which were of lesser moment or which were of frequent and almost daily occurrence, such as the laws prescribing the daily recitation of the canonical hours and the observance of ecclesiastical fasts.[60] In view of the exact words of the present law in canon 81, it must be admitted that any presumed concession is ruled out. Canon 81 clearly shows that the only source of inferior ordinaries' dispensatory power over the general laws

[59] Brys, "De potestate Episcoporum dispensandi in legibus Ecclesiae generalibus," *Collationes Brugenses*, XXIX (1929), 146.

[60] Suarez, *De legibus*, VI, c. 14, n. 9; De Justis, *De Dispensationibus Matrimonialibus*, II, c. 2, nn. 68, 69; D'Annibale, *Summula Theologiae Moralis*, I, n. 231.

of the Church is an express communication of the same, made by a competent superior; and there can be no doubt that these matters —concerning which these older authors maintained a presumed concession of power—must be classified as general laws of the Church. The obligation of reciting the canonical hours and the persons on whom this obligation rests are clearly defined in canons 135, 610 §§ 1, 3, and 1475. The laws of fast and abstinence are embodied in canons 1250-1254. Accordingly, in the absence of an explicit or an implicit grant, ordinaries possess no power over these lesser and frequently occurring matters.

2. Difficult Recourse In An Emergency.

In her customary pastoral solicitude for the welfare of the souls entrusted to her the Church has wisely taken into account the possibility that harm might result for one or more of these souls if a situation should arise which warrants immediate dispensation and at the same time the ordinary were to find himself devoid of any express faculty whereby he might provide for the emergency.[61] Accordingly, she has made the reasonable and explicit concession that ordinaries are empowered to grant any dispensation which the Holy See itself is wont to grant, if a situation is present in which it would be difficult to have recourse to the Holy See to obtain the required dispensation and at the same time there is danger of grave harm in delay.[62] By the terms of this faculty the Church avoids at once both the neglect of her pastoral office and too lavish a concession of power which fundamentally belongs to the Holy See alone.

It might be added in passing that, in accordance with canon 197, § 1, whenever the conditions of canon 81 are fulfilled, the power which is given to ordinaries is ordinary jurisdiction. Therefore, the ordinary "can delegate this power, either totally or in part, unless the law expressly states otherwise." [63]

[61] Brys, "De potestate Episcoporum dispensandi in legibus Ecclesiae generalibus," *Collationes Brugenses,* XXIX, (1929), 144-145.

[62] Can. 81. Cf. also Suarez, *De legibus,* VI, c. 14, n. 10; Sanchez, *De Matrimonio,* lib. II, disp. 40, n. 3.

[63] Can. 199. § 1. Cf. also Litt. Encycl. S.C.S. Off., Mar. 1, 1889—*Collect. S. C. de Prop. Fide,* n. 1698.

In the extraordinary situation for which the Church intends to make provision, all of the three mentioned conditions must concur, namely, a) recourse to the Holy See must be difficult, b) there must be danger of grave harm in delay, c) the dispensation must be one which the Holy See is wont to grant.

a) *Difficulty of recourse to the Holy See.* In this regard an ordinary need consider only one means of having recourse, namely, that of sending to the Holy See a letter containing a petition for the necessary dispensation or for the required faculty to dispense. Accordingly, if he finds it difficult to send such a letter or reasonably concludes that a letter of this kind will not bring a reply from Rome in time to avert the grave danger which threatens, he is thereby empowered to dispense, provided, of course, the other necessary conditions are fulfilled. This statement that an ordinary need take into account only an application by letter is based on the fact that, by the choice of the Holy See, this is the ordinary means of communication with it. Certainly an ordinary is not obliged to make use of the telephone or of a telegram. For not only has the Holy See indicated that there is no such obligation, but it has also pointed out that it disapproves of recourse which is instituted through such means.[64]

Furthermore, although there has been no pertinent explicit declaration of the Holy See, it seems reasonable to conclude that neither is there an obligation to consider the use of other means—such as a journey to Rome by rail or automobile to present the petition—which in one or the other case would not constitute an extraordinary inconvenience for the petitioner, either because of his leisure and financially favorable circumstances or because the petitioner is only a comparatively short distance from Rome. For, while granting that the use of such means in modern circumstances might even be regarded as ordinary means of communication as far as a particular individual is concerned, nevertheless, there is apparently no indication on the part of the Holy See to the

[64] Litt. Encycl. Secret. Status, Dec. 10, 1891—*Collect. S. C. de Prop. Fide,* n. 1775; S. C. S. Off., Aug. 24, 1892—*Fontes,* n. 1159; Commiss. Interp. Cod., Nov. 12, 1922—AAS., XIV (1922), 662.

effect that as far as It is concerned such a method of recourse would not also be regarded as extraordinary. In other words, there is no indication that the Holy See considers as "ordinary" any means of communication other than that of correspondence by letter, even though one could conceive of another method of communication which would in general, as well as in particular, not be extraordinarily inconvenient.

This conclusion can be derived from the following line of reason, deduced from canon 81 itself. Laws in general are enacted in accordance with what is ordinary and common to all for whom they are established.[65] Accordingly, when in canon 81 the legislator uses the term "recourse," it can be presumed that he is referring to the ordinary manner of instituting a recourse, that is, by means of a letter. Moreover, since he indicates no exception, his law is applicable to all cases in which recourse through the medium of a letter is difficult. Evidently the law is intended to provide a remedy precisely for all such instances. Therefore, the canon must be interpreted as though it read "recourse through a letter," even when there is question of that relatively small class who might be able to employ another means of communication without thereby experiencing an extıaordinary inconvenience.

Another question, which can be raised relative to the use of the term "recourse," is whether the term should be understood as being limited to a letter sent directly and personally by the ordinary who is principally concerned; in other words, whether it should be considered as extraordinary—and hence not an obligatory means of communication—if, because of circumstances peculiar to the ordinary, he could easily institute recourse only by employing the agency of another person, either to prepare and send the petition in the ordinary's name, or else to act as an intermediary through whom the ordinary can indirectly communicate with the Holy See. Such a condition might be exemplified in the case of an ordinary who has sustained an injury which prevents him from personally sending the necessary petition; or in the case of an ordinary who, because of the civil authorities'

[65] Cappello, *Summa*, I, n. 125.

opposition to him individually and their interference with his communications with the Holy See, cannot without difficulty recur personally and directly to Rome, but who might be left free either to have someone else recur for him, or to send his petition to a third person who will forward it to the Holy See.

Although it must be admitted that the present law was established primarily to provide for the diffiuclty of an ordinary's personal and direct recourse—because recourse of this kind is the common thing—it seems that its meaning is not limited to this type of communication, since the canon does not state, nor is it implied in the law or in the practice of the Holy See, that recourse must be made personally and directly by the one concerned. Therefore, if, as described above, the obstacles to an ordinary's own direct communication with the Roman Curia are peculiar to him and not common to all, so that he can easily recur mediately through others, the present condition of the canon would not be fulfilled. If, on the contrary, the employment of an intermediary involves danger, for example, of personal harm to the ordinary of the petitioner or danger of the violation of a secret, the ordinary would of course not be obliged to attempt the use of such indirect recourse, because the canon's requirement would then be verified.

With respect to the *difficulty* of recourse—the law does not require that recourse be impossible—it is first of all to be noted that it must be considered with reference to the time which might be allowed to elapse before the reasonably feared harm will arise. That is, one need not consider whether, absolutely speaking, it is difficult to recur to the Holy See, but rather whether recourse can be made and a reply be received in time to avert the threatening harm.

Such a difficulty of recourse is present if "recourse should give rise to grave inconvenience, provided this is not due to fraud or malicious intent on the part of the person instituting said recourse." [66] It can arise from numerous causes, either in ordinary or in extraordinary times; and it might be common to all or re-

[66] Cicognani-O'Hara-Brennan, *Canon Law*, p. 838.

stricted to one or the other individual. In ordinary times, for example, it might be difficult, or even impossible, to apply to the Holy See in time to avert some grave harm, because of the great distance which separates a particular place from Rome, or because of the infrequent collection and delivery of mail in outlying territories. In extraordinary times, such as during a war or in time of persecution, civil authorities might place obstacles in the way of free or fast communication with the Holy See, or the very circumstances of such troublous times might delay the transmission of mail to or from the Holy See. During either ordinary or extraordinary times the difficulty produced by causes such as those just mentioned may be experienced by all in general, or, as already indicated in reference to the method of recourse, it might be limited to one or the other individual. It has also been pointed out that, at least ordinarily, the difficulty will have to be common in order that a concession be made of the power contained in the last part of canon 81. If it is not common, the ordinary who experiences the difficulty might commission, for example, his vicar general or the chancellor to institute the recourse for him.

Moreover, the only recourse which need be considered is specifically recourse to the Holy See, prescinding from the possibility of approaching someone close at hand, the Apostolic Delegate for instance, who might possess the necessary dispensatory power. In other words, if an ordinary finds that recourse to the Holy See is difficult and the other conditions are present, he is empowered to grant the required dispensation, even though he could very easily approach the Apostolic Delegate for the dispensation—under the supposition, of course, that the Delegate has the necessary faculty. An example in point would be with reference to a dispensation from the matrimonial impediment of disparity of worship, when the non-Catholic party is a Jew or a Mohammedan. The granting of such a dispensation is not included in the faculties given to the bishops of the United States, but it is contained in the Apostolic Delegate's.[67] If a situation arises

[67] Cf. Bouscaren, *The Canon Law Digest,* (Milwaukee: Bruce Publishing Co., Vol. I [1934], Vol. II [1937]), II, 7; Vermeersch- Creusen, *Epitome,* I, 525, n. 30.

in which an ordinary can reasonably fear that grave harm will result if the marriage must be postponed for the length of time required for him to have recourse to the Holy Office, he himself can grant the dispensation without having recourse to the Apostolic Delegate.

b) *Danger of grave harm in delay.* Inasmuch as the law makes no distinction with respect to the kind of harm which threatens—other than that it be truly grave, i. e., notable—it can be concluded that a reasonable fear of any grave harm suffices, whether it be physical or moral, public or private, or even economic. Furthermore, an already incurred injury is not necessary. Rather, there is required only a reasonable probability that a grave injury may result if someone must wait until a dispensation can be obtained from the Holy See. The ordinary, on whose conscientious judgment the decision rests, is justified in using his power, if from a consideration of the special circumstances of the individual case he has a positive doubt whether a grave harm will result from the delay.[68]

c) Wont of the Holy See to grant the dispensation in question. It has been indicated earlier that, although all merely ecclesiastical laws are susceptible of dispensation, nevertheless there are some laws which the Holy See never relaxes or from which it dispenses only very rarely and in very extraordinary circumstances. Such laws as are included in these last two classes are outside the category of those which the Holy See is wont to relax, and accordingly can not be relaxed by ordinaries even if the other conditions of canon 81 are present. It would be unreasonable if ordinaries were authorized to relax laws from which the Holy See itself usually does not dispense, especially in view of the fact that the laws which fall into this category are those which

[68] Michiels, *Normae Generales,* II. 484; Brys, "De potestate Episcoporum dispensandi in legibus Ecclesiae generalibus," *Collationes Brugenses,* XXIX (1929), 147; Cicognani-O'Hara-Brennan, *Canon Law.* p. 839; A Coronata, *Institutiones,* I, 107; Toso, *Commentaria Minora,* I, 100.

approximate the divine law or which are more naturally concerned with the common good.[69]

Only from the *stylus* of the Roman Curia can one deduce an enumeration of the Church's laws which are practically indispensable. It includes such laws as those which establish the matrimonial impediments of crime arising from public and notorious conjugicide; of consanguinity in the first degree of the collateral line; of affinity in the direct line if the marriage from which it arises has been consummated; of the sacred order of priesthood; and likewise the law establishing the irregularity *ex defectu corporis* when there is question of an enormous defect.[70]

According to one opinion prior to the Code,[71] another condition was added to those already mentioned for the concession of this power to ordinaries, namely, that the law from which the dispensation was to be granted must be one of lesser moment or of frequent occurrence. Since the Code makes no mention of this condition, its fulfillment is no longer required.

If it should happen that the emergency develops after the ordinary has had recourse to the Holy See but before he has received a reply, and if at the same time he judges that the reply will not be received in time to avert the harm which, it is feared, will result, then the ordinary acts within his rights if he dispenses according to the conditions of canon 81. Elsewhere the Code states that "the non-judicial power of an inferior is not suspended by the mere fact that someone passes by the inferior and has recourse to the superior." [72] For a stronger reason the inferior's power is not suspended if, as in the case under consideration, the subject does not pass by the inferior ordinary, but rather approaches the superior through that inferior.

[69] Toso, *Commentaria Minora,* (2 ed., Romae: Marietti, 1921), I, 181.

[70] Pius X, *Ordo Servandus,* Sept. 29, 1908, *Normae Peculiares,* c. CII, art. III, n. 20—*AAS.,* I (1909), 91; Toso, *Commentaria Minora,* I, 181; Augustine, *A Commentary,* I, 177; Michiels, *Normae Generales,* II, 484; Cicognani-O'Hara-Brennan, *Canon Law,* p. 839; Brys, "De potestate Episcoporum dispensandi in legibus Ecclesiae generalibus," *Collationes Brugenses,* XXIX (1929), 148.

[71] Cf. S. Alphonsus, *Theologia Moralis,* I, n. 190.

[72] Can. 204, § 1.

A doubt might arise concerning the validity of a local ordinary's dispensation granted, when such an emergency occurs, after the recourse has been made but before the reply is received, if later, upon receipt of the Holy See's rescript it is discovered that the dispensation had already been refused by the Roman dicastery at the moment when the ordinary granted it. The doubt would come from the fact that canon 43 suspends the local ordinary's power validly to grant a favor which has been denied by a Sacred Congregation or Office of the Roman Curia, unless that Congregation or Office has consented to his concession of the favor.

When such a case occurs, however, the doubt should be resolved in favor of the validity of the ordinary's dispensation. For, inasmuch as rescripts other than those by which a favor is granted without the intervention of an executor take effect only from the time of execution,[73] the Holy See's refusal of the dispensation will really be subsequent, rather than antecedent, to the ordinary's concession of it. In other words, considering the case as described, one can conclude that the deprivation of a local ordinary's power validly to dispense is not effected, because the conditions do not correspond to those contemplated by canon 43. Moreover, the spirit of the law embodied in canon 43 is apparently that of preventing a local ordinary from knowingly acting contrary to the will of the Holy See. In fine, it can be said in support of the validity of the present use of power that the general tenor of the Code lends itself to the conviction that a person is not dispossessed of his power or authority until he is apprized of this deprival, whether the deprivation is effected in accordance with the law itself or whether it is brought about by the special act of a superior.[74]

[73] Can. 38.

[74] Cf., as a parallel example, canon 192, § 3, relative to a cleric's deprivation of office. Cf. also can. 78, in which the implication is that, although a person deserves to be deprived of a privilege if he abuses the power given to him through that privilege, nevertheless he is not in reality deprived of it until he has been notified to that effect.

3. Relation Of Canon 81 (last part) To Other Canons Containing Explicit Concession Of Power

There is a divergence of opinion among authors concerning the extent of the last part of canon 81 which deals with the power to dispense in urgent cases. Some canonists maintain that a limitation is placed upon the use of the general concession contained therein with respect to those matters in which the legislator has explicitly granted a dispensatory faculty. Thus, in the case of matrimonial dispensations—and this is the only instance of any practical moment—these authors assert that the special concession of canon 1045 is an all-exclusive *(taxativa)* application and determination of the general concession contained in the last part of canon 81, so that the power to dispense from matrimonial impediments in urgent cases cannot be extended beyond the limits of canon 1045, which grants to local ordinaries the power to dispense if "the impediment is discovered when all preparations have been made for the marriage, and the marriage cannot be postponed, without probable danger of grave harm, until the dispensation can be obtained from the Holy See." [75] In the opinion of these authors the indication of the circumstances in canon 1045 designates what alone constitutes an urgent case, outside the danger of death, which latter case is provided for in canon 1043.

Others more correctly maintain that since this provision of canon 81 is so general in character it applies to all ecclesiastical laws and all cases not expressly excepted. They base their contention on the principle that a general concession extends to all the species, unless an express exception is made concerning one or the other of these species.[76] In applying this line of reasoning

[75] De Smet, "Circa dispensandi potestatem apud Ordinarium," *Ephemerides Theologicae Lovanienses,* II (1925), 58; Farrugia, *De Matrimonio et Causis Matrimonialibus* (Taurini-Romae: Marietti, 1924), pp. 165-166; Wernz-Vidal, *Ius Canonicum* (Romae: apud aedes Universitatis Gregorianae, 1925), V, 499.

[76] Brys, "De potestate Episcoporum dispensandi in legibus Ecclesiae generalibus," *Collationes Brugenses,* XXIX (1929), 147; S. D'Angelo. "In can. 1045 Codicis I. C. excursus," *Apollinaris,* I (1928), 260-261; Cap-

to matrimonial dispensations they conclude that ordinaries have the power to dispense even though all preparations for the marriage have not been completed, provided that the three conditions of canon 81 are fulfilled, namely, 1) that recourse to the Holy See is difficult; 2) that there is danger of grave harm in delay; and 3) that the dispensation is one which the Holy See is wont to grant. This course of reasoning, while in itself it is conclusive, will receive added force from a refutation of the reasons offered in support of the opposite opinion. And in this regard it will suffice to give a statement of only those reasons which carry the most force.

1. The first argument is based on the use of the particle *aut* in canon 81, which establishes three sources of power, namely, a) an explicit concession, b) an implicit concession, and c) the presence of an urgent case. This last source is separated from the other two by the word *aut,* which, it is claimed, disjoins two members of a proposition or two propositions which are opposed one to the other. Consequently, the sense of the canon would be that an ordinary receives power *either* from an express concession *or* from the presence of an urgent case; and the concession contained in the latter cannot be extended to a matter in which an explicit concession is made, such as in canon 1045.

Granting, at least for the sake of discussion, that the particle *aut* does produce this effect if the required conditions of canon 1045 are not verified, the ordinary can still dispense provided the conditions of canon 81 are present. Such a use of power would not be an extension of the third source of power (urgent case) to the first source (explicit concession), since in the supposition an explicit concession is lacking by reason of the fact that the explicit grant of canon 1045 is made only if the required circumstances are present, i. e., when all preparations have been made.

2. It is further alleged that canon 1045 would be useless if canon 81 were to include urgent cases in which a matrimonial dispensation is necessary. And since useless laws cannot be pre-

pello, *Tractatus Canonico-Moralis de Sacramentis* (2 ed., Romae: Marietti, 1927), III, n. 234 ad 8; Michiels, *Normae Generales,* II, 485-486.

sumed, the legislator wills to limit the general principle if a special law is present in a legal system.[77] The uselessness of canon 1045 would not, however, necessarily follow from such an interpretation of canon 81. For, while the extent of power in canon 81 is broader than that of canon 1045 with regard to the circumstances in which it can be employed—the former concerns in a general way any emergency; the latter, only the case in which all preparations have been made for the marriage—it is more restricted than canon 1045 as far as the object is concerned. Canon 1045 empowers the local ordinary to dispense from all ecclesiastical matrimonial impediments except those arising from the sacred order of priesthood and from affinity in the direct line, *consummato matrimonio*. Canon 81 on the other hand extends only to those laws which the Apostolic See is wont to relax.[78] Therefore, even when canon 81 is thus interpreted, the presence of canon 1045 will be justified in cases which involve such impediments as those arising from the sacred order of deaconship, age, abduction and forceful retention or finally public and notorious conjugicide—none of which is included under the prescriptions of canon 81.

3. The most cogent reason set forth to prove that canon 1045 restricts the use of the power granted in the last part of canon 81 is derived from the Decree *Proximi Sacra* of the Sacred Consistorial Congregation,[79] in which it was stated that "concerning matrimonial dispensations, although Ordinaries can grant opportune dispensations by reason of canons 1043-1045, . . . nevertheless, his Holiness [Benedict XV] . . . has decreed that these are further *(ulterius)* to be granted: . . . that the same Ordinaries [i.e., of remote places] can dispense for five years from impediments of a major degree . . . which are of ecclesiastical law (except the impediments arising from the sacred order of priesthood and from affinity in the direct line, *consummato matrimonio)*, and also from the impedient impediment of mixed religion, if

[77] Farrugia, *De Matrimonio,* p. 166.

[78] *Supra,* p. 77.

[79] Apr. 25, 1918—*AAS.*, X (1918), 190-192.

a petition for the dispensation has been sent to the Holy See and, pending recourse, an urgent necessity for dispensing supervenes." Evidently this was a temporary concession extending *(ulterius)* the circumstances, in which the dispensations could be granted, so as to include an urgent necessity which might arise when as yet it could not be said that *canonically* all the preparations for a marriage were completed—which concession ceased with the expiration of the time for which it was granted.[80] And since it does constitute an extension it might be construed to imply that canon 81 does not extend to a case of urgent need for a dispensation, if there is question of a matrimonial dispensation. Otherwise canon 81 would have sufficiently provided for these other urgent circumstances and it would not have been necessary for the Roman Pontiff to make the special concession in this decree.

It must be remembered, however, that the pertinent section of the decree refers exclusively to canons 1043 and 1045, and not to the whole Code.[81] Hence the term *ulterius* indicates only that this temporary concession is an extension of the powers which the Code *in this place* grants with regard to matrimonial dispensations.

Moreover, the broader interpretation of canon 81 would not have forestalled the possibility of a practical advantage to be gained for the special concession in the decree. For, while it would provide for the urgent circumstances considered in the decree, it would not have provided as completely as did the special concession, since some of the dispensations which could be granted in virtue of the decree are outside the scope of canon 81, which is limited to those which the Holy See is accustomed to grant.

[80] Wernz-Vidal, *Ius Canonicum,* V, 499-500; S. D'Angelo, "In can. 1045 Codicis I. C. excursus," *Appollinaris,* I (1928), 259. Cf. further decrees of the S. C. Consist. for prorogations of this special concession: Mar. 4, 1919—*AAS.,* XI (1919), 120; March 7, 1921—*AAS.,* XIII (1921), 134.

[81] S. D'Angelo, "In can. 1045 Codicis I. C. excursus," *Apollinaris,* I (1928), 261.

4. Custom As a Source Of Dispensatory Power

A consideration of the sources of derived dispensatory power must take into account the possibility of such power arising from custom, since one can conceive of an implicit concession based on a lawfully prescribed custom. Some authors [82] contend that it is scarcely possible to conceive of a *legitimate* custom in this regard, because a practice of this kind would not fulfill the requirements for a custom of law, namely, that it must be induced by the actions of a *community* which is capable of receiving a law.[83] The canon on which these canonists base their contention, however, is concerned with those customs which result in an obligation incumbent upon the community to observe them. But there is another kind of custom—usually termed *factual*—which consists merely in a uniformity of action in a certain matter, protracted over a period of time.[84] Such a custom does not of necessity give rise to an obligation, and accordingly does not fall within the terms of canon 26. It can, moreover, be induced by the repeated uniform actions either of a community or of an individual, and if it fulfills the two conditions of (1) duration of prescribed time and (2) at least tacit consent of the competent superior, it can effect a facultative right.

The opinion of those authors who maintain that custom can be a source of power whereby ordinaries can dispense from the Church's laws [85] is not without solid foundation, at least if the principle is limited to immemorial and centenary customs. For, in an instruction of the Holy Office,[86] which has apparently never

[82] Cappello, *Summa,* I, n. 127 ad 8; Michiels, *Normae Generales,* II, 487.

[83] Can. 26: "Communitas quae legis ecclesiasticae saltem recipiendae capax est, potest consuetudinem inducere quae vim legis obtineat."

[84] Guilfoyle, *Custom,* (The Catholic University of America, Canon Law Studies, n. 105, Washington: The Catholic University of America, 1937), p. 78.

[85] Suarez, *De legibus,* VI, c. 14, n. 10; Bouix, *Tractatus de Episcopo,* II, 93; De Justis, *De Dispensationibus Matrimonialibus,* lib. II, c. 2, n. 60; Brys, "De potestate Episcoporum dispensandi in legibus Ecclesiae generalibus," *Collationes Brugenses,* XXIX (1929), 149.

[86] June 8, 1756—*Collect. S. C. de Prop. Fide,* I, n. 399: " . . . Sola itaque Apostolicae Sedis facultas, vel, praeter hanc, immemorabilis

been abrogated, immemorial and centenary customs are mentioned as productive of power to dispense from public diriment matrimonial impediments. And although it is evident that this Instruction refers only to matrimonial impediments, it indicates that the Holy See recognizes as valid the dispensatory acts of ordinaries performed in virtue of a custom which has continued in its practice from time immemorial or for a whole century.

With the foregoing Instruction as a norm, one can conclude that an ordinary custom of forty years' duration [87] does not give rise to such dispensatory power, but that an immemorial custom or one which has existed for at least a hundred years yields this power, if, of course, at least tacit consent of the superior is present.[88]

Naturally, this attribution of dispensatory power cannot be so extensive as to include the power to relax a law which the Holy See is not wont to dispense, because it would be unreasonable to suppose that in ordinary circumstances an inferior could make a concession which the supreme authority itself would not grant.

5. Limitation Of Ordinaries' Dispensatory Power By Reason Of Previous Refusal Of Dispensation

Restrictions, similar to the limitation of power with reference to the Congregations and Offices of the Roman Curia,[89] are to be found in canons 43 and 44 with respect to the dispensatory power of inferior ordinaries. These two canons consider four different sets of circumstances and determine the effect which the refusal of a dispensation by one superior has on the subsequent concession made by another superior. These canons use the term "favor," but for the present purposes it will be advantageous to substitute the term "dispensation," since it is this type of favor only which is concerned here.

consuetudo aut saltem centenaria, unde posset Romani Pontificis benignus assensus legitime deprehendi, dispensationem in publicis impedimentis dirimentibus reddere potest validam."

[87] Can. 27.

[88] Can. 25.

[89] *Supra*, p. 62.

The first case considered is one in which the refusal has been made by one of the Congregations or Offices of the Roman Curia. When the request for a dispensation has been thus denied, a local ordinary, even though otherwise he possesses the necessary power, cannot validly grant the desired dispensation without the consent of the dicastery which has refused it.[90] It is worthy of note that canon 43 expressly uses the phrase "local ordinary." Consequently, since according to canon 19 a strict interpretation must be given to canon 43, the same invalidity is not present if a dispensation is subsequently granted by an ordinary who is not a local ordinary, for example, by a major superior of an exempt clerical institute.[91]

The circumstances contemplated in the second case are those in which a dispensation has been refused by one's own ordinary and later it is requested of another competent ordinary, who is jurisdictionally on the same plane with one's own ordinary. For example, with respect to a dispensation from the law of fast and abstinence a *peregrinus* can request the dispensation either from the ordinary of his domicile or quasi-domicile, or from the ordinary of the place where he is sojourning. The pertinent law, established to protect within reason the authority of the person's proper ordinary, is the following: "No one shall ask another ordinary for a favor [dispensation] refused by his own ordinary, without making known the refusal; if the refusal is mentioned, the [second] ordinary shall not grant the favor until he has been informed by the first ordinary of his reasons for refusal." [92]

The failure to observe this law, either on the part of the petitioner or on the part of the granter does not, however, affect the validity of a dispensation granted in contravention of the law,[93] but it naturally renders such a concession unlawful.

In accordance with the strict interpretation which must be given to this law,[94] certain sets of circumstances which bear a

[90] Can. 43.

[91] Chelodi, *Ius de Personis*, p. 128, nota 1; Cappello, *Summa*, I, 155-156.

[92] Can. 44, § 1.

[93] Can. 11.

[94] Can. 19.

resemblance to those considered in the canon are nevertheless outside of the embrace of this law and consequently do not affect even the lawfulness of the concession. Thus, a person may seek a dispensation from an ordinary other than his own and if it is refused he may request it of his own ordinary. In this case the latter is not bound to seek the former's reasons for the refusal, but can freely grant the dispensation if he sees fit to do so. Nor is it forbidden later to seek a dispensation, without mentioning the previous denial, from the same ordinary who previously refused it, or from his successor.[95]

Finally, the canon does not oblige the second ordinary to defer to the reasons of the proper ordinary. Once he has been informed of these reasons by the person's own ordinary, he can proceed to grant the dispensation if he judges that a sufficiently just and reasonable cause is present.

The third consideration is that of the effect of a vicar-general's refusal on the subsequent concession of a dispensation by the bishop. In order that a bishop's relaxation of a law under these circumstances may be valid, it is necessary that mention be made to him of the fact that the dispensation has previously been refused by the vicar-general.[96] The reason underlying this law is the fact that a bishop and his vicar-general are regarded as constituting a single juridical personality, which should function, so to speak, as a single person, in the sense that there should be no unreasonable conflict or disagreement on matters which are subject to the jurisdiction of the bishop and of the vicar-general alike. And since this is so, the supreme legislator declares the invalidity of a dispensation in the present circumstances, not because the necessary power is lacking, but on the strength of the legal presumption that the bishop does not will to grant a dispensation which his vicar-general has refused to concede. Naturally, this presumption gives way if the bishop wills otherwise. If the bishop dispenses after being informed of the vicar-general's refusal, or if he should say that he wills to grant a

[95] A Coronata, *Institutiones*, I, 62; Michiels, *Normae Generales*, II, 182.
[96] Can. 44, § 2.

certain dispensation regardless of whether the vicar-general has previously refused it, his will prevails and the dispensation is valid.[97]

In both the present case and the following one it is understood that the law refers to the bishop and vicar-general of one and the same diocese. Else, it would not be possible to assign the underlying reason for the legislation, namely, the special relation which exists between the two superiors. Wherefore, if the bishop or vicar-general of a diocese were to refuse the request of one who is not strictly a subject of that diocese, the person in question could validly obtain the dispensation from the bishop or vicar-general of his own diocese, even without mentioning the previous refusal.[98]

The fourth case is the converse of the third. It deals with a bishop's refusal of a dispensation and the effect which such a refusal exercises on his vicar-general's power to grant the same dispensation. The law provides that if a dispensation has been refused by a bishop, his vicar-general cannot validly grant the same, even if the previous refusal is made known to him, unless the bishop gives his consent to the granting of the dispensation.[99] This prescription is based on the nature of the vicar-general's office. A vicar-general is appointed for the purpose of assisting the bishop in the correct government of the diocese.[100] The judgment concerning what is to the best interests of the souls of the diocese rests principally with the bishop, whose judgment should not be contradicted by that of his vicar-general. The Code expressly declares this when it says that the vicar-general "shall avoid using his powers contrary to the mind and will of the bishop."[101] A bishop's refusal to grant a certain dispensation

[97] Cappello, *Summa,* I, n. 147; Cicognani-O'Hara-Brennan, *Canon Law*, pp. 723-724; Michiels, *Normae Generales,* II, 183.

[98] Bouuaert-Simenon, *Manuale Juris Canonici,* I, 117; Cappello, *Summa,* I, n. 147; Michiels, *Normae Generales,* II, 182, nota 3; Vermeersch-Creusen, Epitome, I, n. 129; A Coronata, *Institutiones,* I, 63.

[99] Can. 44, § 2.

[100] Can. 366, § 1.

[101] Can. 369, § 2.

is an expression of his will that the subject who requests it should not be thus favored. Consequently, the vicar-general's will to dispense in the same case would be to no avail, since it would be in contravention of the will of the bishop, who must be presumed to withhold from the vicar-general all power that would enable the latter to act against the will of the bishop.

6. Derived Power Enjoyed Only By Local Ordinaries

In addition to the proper dispensatory power which the principal ordinaries can exercise over diocesan laws,[102] and the derived dispensatory power which they enjoy with regard to general laws of the Church, canon 82 confers on each local ordinary of the territory over which the jurisdiction of the particular council extends, the authority to relax, in accordance with canon 291, § 2, that is, "in particular cases and for a just cause," the laws enacted by plenary or provincial councils.

Unless the jurisdictional nature of these particular councils—and hence the nature of their laws—is correctly understood, it might appear that the phrase "except in particular cases and for a just cause" constitutes a restriction of the local ordinary's power, based solely on the positive will of the supreme legislator. On the contrary, it is a *concession* of dispensatory power, based solely on the expression of the legislator's will, since the local ordinary possesses no inherent authority to relax laws enacted by such councils.

If the nature of these councils were such that their power was merely the sum total of the jurisdiction residing separately in those assembled in the council, the conciliar laws would, in reality, be nothing more than diocesan laws uniformly established for the various dioceses whose superiors participated in the

[102] What was said above (p. 57) is to be recalled in this connection, namely, that while the vicar-general of a residential bishop, of an Abbot *nullius*, or of a prelate *nullius*, or the *vicarius delegatus* of a mission territory, enjoys the power to dispense from the laws enacted by his respective principal ordinary or his predecessor, his power is not proper but vicarious.

council.[103]—which the individual ordinaries could relax in accordance with what has already been said concerning diocesan laws. This follows from the fact that the jurisdiction of the individual local ordinary does not extend beyond the confines of his territory. Wherefore, even if two or more of these local ordinaries *as local ordinaries* unite, they cannot enact laws for the larger territory which will bind the various legislators themselves.[104]

A council, however, is by its nature a collegiate group whose participants are assembled not as local ordinaries or superiors of lesser territories, but *as members of the collegiate body*—a group on which the supreme legislator has bestowed jurisdiction superior to that possessed personally and separately by the members of the group. To this jurisdiction the individual local ordinaries are subject. The legislator in a council is not any one of the assembled members, but the *coetus episcoporum.*[105] In accordance, therefore, with the fundamental principle embodied in canon 80, and for the reason that such conciliar laws are of a superior authority, inferiors enjoy dispensatory power over them only in so far as this power is expressly communicated to them. It is such a concession which canon 82 makes in favor of local ordinaries in particular cases and for a just cause.

It would not, however, be contrary to the prescription of canon 291, § 2, if the council itself were to include in the promulgation of its decrees a concession of power beyond that which the Code gives to local ordinaries, especially in view of the fact that before the acts and decrees of a plenary or of a provincial council are promulgated they must be censored by the Holy See.[106] Canon 291 is not intended to be a restriction of the principles contained, for example, in canons 80 and 199, § 1. Rather, it would seem that the Church desires to insure for the local ordinaries at least that minimum of power over particular conciliar decrees, leaving the

[103] Suarez, *De legibus,* VI, c. 15, nn. 2—4; Wernz, *Jus Decretalium,* I, 264; Chelodi, *Ius de Personis,* p. 364.

[104] Chelodi, *Ius de Personis* p. 364.

[105] Suarez, *De legibus,* VI, c. 15, n. 4; Wernz, *Jus Decretalium,* I, 263-264; Chelodi, *Ius de Personis,* p. 364.

[106] Can, 291, § 1.

conciliar legislators free to increase that power if they so choose.

The final clause of canon 82 excludes from the competence of local ordinaries the granting of a dispensation from laws especially enacted for that particular territory by the Roman Pontiff unless in accordance with canon 81 they have received an explicit or an implicit faculty, or unless recourse to the Holy See is difficult and there is danger of grave harm in delay.

In his commentary on this clause, a Coronata makes an apparently unwarranted distinction between particular laws established by particular decrees of the Roman Congregations and those laws which the Roman Pontiff has established for a particular territory, thereby implying that the particular laws of the Congregations fall within the competence of local ordinaries.[107] While it is evident that the canon does not make explicit mention of laws enacted by the Holy See, it must be remembered that any law emanating from the Holy See participates in the nature of a papal law, since the power of the Congregations and Offices of the Roman Curia is vicarious, rather than delegated, and accordingly is exercised in the name and on the authority of the Roman Pontiff.[108]

There is, moreover, the consideration which cannot be overlooked, namely, that even though these laws are truly particular, the authority on which they are based is superior to the local ordinary's; and, as has been shown above, the mind of the Church is that an inferior cannot dispense a superior's law unless he has received an express concession—whether this concession is explicit or only implicit. But the basis on which a Coronata places his implied attribution of power to local ordinaries, that is, on the fact that the canon uses the words *quas speciatim tulerit*

[107] A Coronata, *Institutiones*, I, 108, nota 5. The opposite opinion is maintained by Augustine, *A. Commentary*, I, 178, and by Blat, *Commentarium Textus Codicis Iuris Canonici*, (Romae: in Instituto Pii IX, 1921). I, 153.

[108] Cf. can. 244; "Dubia circa facultates dispensandi ab impedimentis matrimonialibus," *AAS.*, VII (1872), pp. 427, 430; Const. Pii X, *Sapienti Consilio*, June 29, 1908—*AAS.*, I (1909), 7-9; Cappello, *Summa*, I, n. 318, ad 3.

Romanus Pontifex and does not explicitly mention laws which are *latae a Sancta Sede*—such a basis could be considered at the very most as a *tacit* bestowal of power. As such, however, it cannot be regarded as sufficient to establish a right whereby a local ordinary can dispense from these particular laws.

D. Parish Priests

Canon 83. Parochi nec a lege generali nec a lege peculiari dispensare valent, nisi haec potestas expresse eisdem concessa sit.

The prescription of canon 83 might well be understood from the principles enunciated in the preceding three canons. But the legislator saw fit to include an explicit declaration of the circumstances under which parish priests can exercise dispensatory power. Perhaps this fact can be attributed to the lack of uniformity in this regard among authors prior to the Code. Some of these canonists maintained that parish priests could, by reason of tacit delegation or custom, dispense in particular cases from the more frequently recurring precepts, for example, from the law of fasting and from the law forbidding servile works on holydays of obligation.[109]

Another opinion attributed to parish priests power similar to that possessed by ordinaries if recourse to the ordinary could not be made to obtain the dispensation and there was danger in delay. The basis of this power was said to be the presumed will of the legislator.[110]

Under the law of the Code it is clear that the only source of dispensatory power is an express concession either from the law or from a competent superior.

Express grants of dispensatory power to parish priests and to those who are included under the term *parochi*[111] are embodied in the following canons of the Code.

[109] Suarez, *De legibus,* VI, c. 14, n. 10; Sanchez, *De Matrimonio,* lib. VIII, disp. 9, n. 27; Wernz, *Jus Decretalium,* I. n. 122.

[110] S. Alphonsus, *Theologia Moralis,* lib. VI, n. 613.

[111] Can. 451, § 2: "1° Quasi-parochi qui quasi-paroecias regunt, de quibus in can. 216, § 3; 2° Vicarii paroeciales, si plena potestate paroeciali sint praediti."

1) canon 1245, § 1—the power to dispense from the observance of holydays, and of fasts, or of abstinence, or of both, not only individual subjects and individual families (even outside their territory), but also *peregrini* who are within the limits of the parish priests' respective territories.

2) canon 1044—in cases involving the danger of death, when recourse to the ordinary is impossible, for relief of conscience and, if the case requires it, for the legitimation of offspring, the power to dispense their own subjects everywhere, and all others actually residing in their respective territories, from the prescribed form of marriage, and from all impediments of ecclesiastical law, except those arising from priesthood and affinity in the direct line once the marriage has been consummated.

3) canon 1045, § 3—in occult cases in which recourse to the ordinary is either impossible or would involve the danger of violation of a secret, the power to dispense their own subjects, and also all who are present in their respective territories, from all ecclesiastical impediments except those arising from priesthood and from affinity in the direct line once the marriage has been consummated, if the impediment is detected after all preparations for the marriage have been made and the marriage cannot be postponed without probable danger of grave harm until a dispensation can be obtained from the Holy See.

Implicit dispensatory power can be acquired by parish priests in the same ways that ordinaries can acquire it, namely, whenever it is necessarily included in an explicit communication of power.

E. Confessors, Minor Religious Superiors, etc.

Although the Code makes no explicit mention in this title of others on whom jurisdiction can be conferred, for example, confessors, minor superiors in clerical exempt religious institutes, or a priest who assists at marriage, it can be deduced from the principles developed above that they likewise possess only such dispensatory power as has been expressly given to them. Consequently, they can grant only those dispensations which they are expressly empowered to grant either by the law itself [112] or in virtue of special or general faculties contained in an indult of a competent superior.

[112] Cf. can. 990, § 2; 1044; 1045; 1245, § 3; 1313; 1320.

CHAPTER VII

THE PASSIVE SUBJECT OF DISPENSATORY POWER

Article I. Requirement of Superior-Subject Relationship

The most fundamental principle underlying the designation of those who can directly receive a dispensation is set forth in canon 201, § 1, which declares that "the power of jurisdiction can be exercised directly only over subjects." [1] Accordingly, a superior-subject relationship must be established before any claim to dispensatory power over an individual person can be substantiated. The basis on which this relationship rests is not the same in every case; rather, it varies in accordance with the extent of the individual superior's jurisdiction.

A. Superior-Subject Relationship in the Internal Forum

The internal forum,—in distinction to the external forum which takes cognizance of affairs relating to the faithful as members of the Church as a society—is concerned with the private sanctification of man and his relationship with God. The workings of this forum regard man's position not before society but before God. It is the *sacramental* internal forum when the question at hand is treated by the confessor in the act of sacramental confession; the *extra-sacramental* internal forum, if the matter is dealt with outside the sacrament of penance, but only with respect to the interested party's standing before God.[2]

In this internal forum the superior-subject relationship, or the so called *titulus subjectionis,* is verified by the penitential char-

[1] One who in all other matters is not a subject of a given superior can indirectly become the subject of his dispensatory power for an individual case by reason of his connection with one who directly receives a dispensation from that superior. Thus, in the case of a relative impediment to a marriage—consanguinity, for example—in which one of the parties is a subject, the other a non-subject, when a competent superior grants a dispensation, he directly dispenses his subject. Indirectly, by that very fact, he relaxes the obligation of the law for the non-subject also.

[2] Pacificus Capobianco, "De notione fori interni in iure canonico," *Apollinaris,* IX (1936), 365-366.

acter of the one who presents himself to a person who is jurisdictionally competent in the internal forum. The penitential character in turn is present *actually* when a person approaches the sacramental forum; *potentially*, if he presents the case to the extra-sacramental internal forum.[3] The sufficiency of this single title is demonstrable from the Code itself.

In the first place, with respect to the sacramental forum, any duly authorized confessor who has the necessary faculty to grant a dispensation, for example, from irregularities arising out of an occult delict,[4] can exercise his jurisdiction in favor of any person who goes to confession to him, irrespective of whether that person possesses a domicile or quasi-domicile in that parish or diocese or whether he belongs to the Latin or to an Oriental rite.[5] In another canon the Code explicitly states the unqualified corresponding right of any one of the faithful to make his confession to any approved confessor.[6] These canons do not have explicit reference to dispensatory power, but they serve to indicate that, in the mind of the Church, and as far as the sacramental forum is concerned, the relationship between any approved confessor and any member of the faithful is the relationship of jurisdictional superior and subject.

Secondly, anyone who possesses jurisdiction for the internal forum can exercise his power in the extra-sacramental internal forum, except in those cases in which it is prescribed that it must be used in the sacramental forum.[7] An example of this kind of restriction is contained in the communication of dispensatory power with regard to matrimonial impediments in danger of death or when all the preparations for marriage have been completed.[8]

[3] Michiels, *Normae Generales*, II, 492; Cappello, *Summa*, I, n. 131.

[4] Can. 990, § 1.

[5] Can. 881, § 1: "Omnes . . . sacerdotes ad audiendas confessiones approbati in aliquo loco . . . possunt etiam vagos ac peregrinos ex alia dioecesi vel paroecia ad sese accedentes, itemque catholicos cuiusque ritus orientalis, valide et licite absolvere."

[6] Can. 905: "Cuivis fideli integrum est confessario legitime approbato etiam alius ritus, cui maluerit, peccata sua confiteri."

[7] Can. 202, § 2.

[8] Can. 1043; 1044; 1045.

Since, therefore, one who has the necessary power can dispense in the sacramental forum any of the faithful who come to him, and since he possesses the same power in the extra-sacramental internal forum—unless the sacramental forum is prescribed—it follows that the superior-subject relationship is established by the mere fact that any of the faithful have recourse to one who is jurisdictionally competent in that extra-sacramental internal forum. In other words, such a priest can grant the requested dispensation, even though in the external forum no such relationship exists.

B. Superior-Subject Relationship in the External Forum

In the external forum three classes of superiors must be distinguished, because the juridical fact by which a person is constituted a subject is different with respect to each of the three classes.

1) The Roman Pontiff. Inasmuch as the jurisdiction of the Roman Pontiff is supreme and co-extensive with the Church, it reaches every member of the Church. Consequently, he can dispense any human being who has received valid baptism, since valid baptism establishes ecclesiastical personality.[9] This can be said as truly of baptized non-Catholics as of Catholics, so that the Pope has power to dispense all alike, although in the customary practice he does not directly and formally dispense non-Catholics.[10]

2) Territorial Superiors, such as local ordinaries, parish priests, etc. The passive subject of the dispensatory power possessed by these territorial superiors is determined, in addition to valid baptism, by possession of a domicile,[11] or of a quasi-domicile,[12] or, in the case of *vagi*, by actual residence [13] in the territory of the one who dispenses. In the first two cases it is possession of the

[9] Can. 12; 87.

[10] Benedictus XIV, Const. *Inter omnigenas*, Feb. 2, 1744— *Collect. S. C. de Prop. Fide*, I, n. 345; Michiels, *Normae Generales*, II, 493; Cappello *De Sacramentis*, III, n, 252.

[11] Can. 92, §§ 1, 3; 94, §§ 1, 3.

[12] Can. 92, §§ 2, 3; 94, §§ 1, 3.

[13] Can. 94, § 2; 91.

domicile or quasi-domicile which establishes the superior-subject relationship and not the actual presence in the territory. Therefore, a person who is temporarily absent from his domicile or quasi-domicile does not cease to be a subject of the superior of that territory and the latter can exercise his dispensatory power in favor of such a subject even when he is outside the territory.[14]

3) Religious Superiors. A person becomes the subject of a religious superior by reason of juridic membership in the community which that superior governs.[15] Thus an individual religious becomes the subject of a local superior by being assigned to the house which that superior governs; all the religious—whether they be local superiors or their subjects—belonging to the various local communities which are united to form a province (or similar division)—if the institute is divided into provinces—are the subjects of the major superior who is placed at the head of the province; and, finally, all members of the institute are the subjects of the institute's Supreme Moderator.[16]

The foregoing designation is based upon the customary hierarchy of superiors in religious institutes. In some instances it will be different, as in the case of monasteries *sui iuris* and monastic congregations. The members of individual monasteries are subject to the respective abbots, but the subjection of the members included in a monastic congregation is not as complete with respect to the *Abbas Primas* and *Superior* as is that of religious of other institutes to their respective major superiors. Except for the powers contained in canons 655 and 1594, § 4, the jurisdiction of the *Abbas Primas* and *Superior* must be determined by the constitutions of the institute and the special decrees of the Holy See.[17]

By an extension of the idea of membership, superiors are, at

[14] Can. 201, § 3: "Nisi aliud ex rerum natura aut ex iure constet, potestatem jurisdictionis voluntariam seu non-iudicialem quis exercere potest . . . extra territorium existens, aut in subditum e territorio absentem."

[15] Michiels, *Normae Generales,* II, 494.

[16] Can. 502

[17] Can. 501, § 3.

times, empowered to dispense others also who, strictly considered, are not members of the religious community, such as those "who live day and night in a religious house either as servants, or for the purpose of education, or as guests, or on account of ill health." [18] Valid baptism is, of course, also presupposed in this regard, just as it is with respect to territorial superiors' jurisdiction.

C. *Peregrini* AS SUBJECTS OF DISPENSATORY POWER

A very moot question among canonists concerns the status of *peregrini* [19] and the possibility of their being regarded as subjects of the dispensatory power of those superiors in whose territory the *peregrini* are acutally staying. In other words, prescinding from any express communication of power granted by a competent superior, and presupposing that materially the particular dispensation is within the limits of the dispensing superior's power,[20] does the common law authorize the superior of a territory to dispense also those "transients" who, it so happens, are in his territory?

Those who answer this question in the negative consider canon 94 as an exclusive determination of subjects and consequently maintain that *peregrini* cannot be classed as true subjects of such a superior. They say, moreover, that the Code's express inclusion of *peregrini* in some particular instances[21] indicates that they are excluded in other cases.[22]

Those who affirm [23] this power with regard to *peregrini* advance the following reasons for their position: 1) no law is to be found which expressly declares that the temporary sojourn of *peregrini*

[18] Can. 514, § 1; 1245, §3.

[19] Can. 91: "Persona dicitur . . . *peregrinus*, si versetur extra domicilium et quasi-domicilium quod adhuc retinet."

[20] Cf. v. g., can. 81; 83; 14, §§ 1, 2.

[21] V. g., can. 1043; 1045; 1245; 1313; 1320.

[22] A Coronata, *Institutiones*, I. n. 113 ad 2°; Chelodi, *Ius de Personis*, p. 145, nota 1.

[23] Bouuaert-Simenon, *Manuale Juris Canonici*, I, 135, n. 233; Cappello, *Summa*, I, n. 130 ad 2°; Michiels, *Normae Generales*, II, 495; Maroto, *Institutiones*, I, 364.

is not sufficient to constitute a *titulus subjectionis* to the superior of that territory. On the contrary, in at least one instance, the subjection of *peregrini* to a superior of the territory is determined by the very fact that they are present in his territory.[24] 2) in view of the milder discipline induced by the Code,[25] it is more in conformity with the spirit of the Code to amplify dispensatory power which is granted in favor of souls in general.[26]

On the strength of these reasons, this opinion must be regarded as at least probable; and since there is evidently a doubt of fact concerning the point at issue, namely, that *peregrini* are to be regarded as subjects with reference to a superior's dispensatory power, the superior can exercise his dispensatory faculty in accordance with canon 15.

D. Use of Dispensatory Power in One's Own Favor

1. The Legislator. A discussion of the possibility of a legislator's dispensation from his own law and in his own behalf must take into consideration the underlying question of whether the legislator is bound by his own law and, if he is bound, the question of the nature of the obligation. First of all, the problem can concern only a case in which an individual physical person is the legislator because, if a collegiate group is the legislator, the single members comprising the group are not severally the legislator. Rather, each individual member is a subject of the jurisdiction exercised by the group. The one exception to this is the relationship between an ecumenical council and the Roman Pontiff who is not so much a member of the council as he is its head.[27]

As far as the *coactive force* of a law is concerned, authors are agreed that the legislator is not bound by his own law, so that

[24] Can. 14, § 1, n. 2°: "Peregrini non adstringuntur legibus territorii in quo versantur, iis exceptis quae ordini publico consulunt, vel actuum solemnia determinant."

[25] Can. 1043, 1045, 1245, 1313, 1320.

[26] Can. 200, § 1.

[27] Noldin, *De Principiis Theologiae Moralis* (18 ed., Oeniponte: Rauch, 1925), p. 151; Van Hove, De Legibus Ecclesiasticus (Mechliniae-Romae: Dessain, 1930), p. 208; Wernz, *Ius Decretalium,* I, 126.

he is not obliged to observe the penal sanctions arising from the non-observance of the law, because the notion of coercion, that is, of passing sentence or of inflicting penalties, presupposes a distinction of persons—which distinction is lacking in the present case.[28]

The legislator is, however, bound by the *preceptive* or *directive force* of his law. In other words, he is obliged to observe the law itself as distinguished from the sanctions of the law. The authors just cited describe this obligation as an indirect bond arising provisionally from the dictates of right reason and the natural law which requires that the legislator promote the common good by the good example of conforming himself to his subjects, at least when the matter of the law is common to both and the same reasons can be advanced for the observance of a law by both the legislator and his subjects. Therefore, given a positive human law, the legislator must observe it.

Relative to the legislator's relaxation of his own law in his own behalf, it can consequently be said that, since the obligation to abide by his law is based on the natural law, there can be no question of a true dispensation. For his lawful non-observance of the law, a cause *excusing* him from its obligation, rather than a dispensation, is required. The obligation of a natural law ceases if the so called *materia legis* is changed. In the present case the "matter" is the promotion of the common good *precisely by the legislator's observance of his own law.* But when a sufficient cause is present for not observing it, this precise matter is altered. Hence, the obligation ceases, inasmuch as the presence of the cause prevents the detriment to the common good which would otherwise result.[29]

[28] S. Thomas, *Summa Theologica,* 1, 2, q. 96, art. 5 ad 3; Noldin, *De Principiis,* p. 151; Van Hove, *De Legibus Ecclesiasticis,* pp. 208-209; Suarez, *De Legibus,* III, c. 35, n. 19; Wernz, *Ius Decretalium,* 1, 126.

[29] Suarez (*De legibus,* VI, c. 19, n. 17) maintains that the power to dispense from one's own law results from the fact that the natural law in question is conditioned in a way which implies that "the legislator should observe his law, unless for a just cause he dispenses himself." This, however, is a gratuitous assertion and is not fortified by solid reasons.

Ordinarily, a more weighty cause is required for an excuse than is required for a dispensation. In the present case, however, a cause which would suffice for granting a dispensation to a subject will likewise be adequate to excuse the legislator, because his obligation is not a grave one and is founded only on the appropriateness of the prescribed conformity with his subjects, not on the particular virtue by reason of which his subjects are bound to the observance of the law.[30]

2. One who has received for the extra-sacramental internal forum or for the external forum [31] a general faculty to dispense from a superior's law can use his power for his own benefit: a) indirectly, either by participating in a dispensation which he grants to the entire community, or by granting to someone else the faculty to dispense him; b) directly, by granting to himself a dispensation. Since this is an employment of voluntary jurisdiction by which a favor is bestowed, it does not require a distinction of persons, such as is required in the exercise of the so-called contentious jurisdiction. The Code itself has further substantitated this doctrine of the authors.[32]

Article II. The Subject's Use of a Dispensation

The act of a competent superior designed to relax a law does not, of necessity, imply that the subject (or subjects) in whose favor the act is performed is *unrestrictedly* at liberty to use the

[30] Michiels, *Normae Generales,* II, 497; Noldin, *De Principiis,* p. 151 ad 3. Cf. Van Hove *(De Legibus Ecclesiasticis,* pp. 210-211), who cites also other authors.

[31] One whose power is restricted to the sacramental forum cannot use his faculty in his own behalf. Otherwise, because of the judicial character of the sacrament of Penance, the case would resolve itself into one of a person's acting as his own judge—which is not permissible, since "judicial power . . . cannot be exercised in one's own behalf." (Can. 201, § 2).

[32] Can. 201, § 3: "Nisi aliud ex rerum natura aut ex iure constet, potestatem iurisdictionis voluntariam seu non-iudicialem quis exercere potest etiam in proprium commodum . . . " Cf. Noldin, *De Principiis,* n. 185; Michiels, *Normae Generales,* II, 497, 498; A Coronata, *Institutiones,* I, 111; Maroto, *Institutiones,* I, 364.

dispensation. For, while the immediate effect of a valid dispensation is the subject's freedom from the obligation of the law, several aspects of the dispensatory act can place limitations on the subject's freedom. The restraining effect produced by some of these aspects is immediately obvious, for example, when the grant has been made conditionally and the condition has not been fulfilled, or when the concession has been given for a limited time and the time designated has elapsed. Other limitations, perhaps slightly less obvious, can arise from:

a) *the validity of the grant.* Naturally, if the superior has acted invalidly, the obligation of the law continues in force, and the subject is not at liberty to act contrary to it. As already indicated in the preceding chapter, this invalidity is present if the superior exceeds the power with which he is endowed; and as will be shown later, it can arise from the absence of a just cause for dispensing. Without, at present, going into the details of the causal requirements, the following rules might be set forth as practical deductions, the reasonableness of which will be evident from the doctrine expressed in the later chapter on cause. 1. When a just cause is present the use of a dispensation is both valid and lawful. 2. If there is no just cause, but one is erroneously thought to exist, as a general rule the dispensation granted (a) by an inferior is certainly invalid, (b) by the legislator, is *presumed* to be invalid, because of lack of intention,[33] and hence cannot be used. The exception to this general rule is the case of a dispensation from a matrimonial impediment of a minor degree. Canon 1054 declares that such a dispensation is not vitiated even though the only final cause alleged should be false.[34] 3. If a just cause actually exists, but the petitioner and the one dispensing erroneously think there is no such cause, the use of the dispensation will be valid from the beginning, because the dispensation itself is valid. The validity of the dispensation depends on the actual existence of a just cause, and not on the dispenser's knowledge of its existence. Moreover, the use of the dispensation will

[33] *Infra*, pp. 111 112.

[34] Cf. O'Mara, *Canonical Causes For Matrimonial Dispensations*, p. 61.

be *lawful,* even though, in the supposition, the petition for and the granting of the dispensation have been illicit. Since, actually, the obligation of the law no longer exists for the recipient of the dispensation, there is no law which forbids his acting in accordance with the dispensation, prescinding, of course, from possible scandal which such a use might entail. 4. When it is known that a just cause is lacking, the use of a dispensation is both invalid and unlawful if the law has been relaxed by one who is inferior to the legislator, since such a dispensation is both invalid and unlawful. But if the legislator makes the concession, it will be valid, since he can and, in the supposition, evidently intends to dispense regardless of the absence of a just cause.[35] The obligation of the law no longer exists for the dispensed person, who is, as a consequence, at liberty to act accordingly. 5. If a dispensation has been granted when a doubt was present concerning either the existence or the sufficiency of a just cause, the concession is both lawful and valid.[36] Therefore, the use of it will likewise be lawful and valid.

b) *the forum in which the concession is made.* Although a dispensation granted in the external forum can be applied also in the internal forum, the opposite is not true.[37] In other words, if a person has been dispensed in the internal forum, whether it be the sacramental forum or the extra-sacramental internal forum, he is not thereby freed from the obligation of the law, as far as the external forum is concerned. There is, however, an exception to this rule when there is question of a dispensation from an occult matrimonial impedient, when the concession has been made in the *extra-sacramental* internal forum. Canon 1047 prescribes that if such a dispensation has been granted, "unless the rescript of the Sacred Penitentiary provides otherwise . . . another dispensation for the external forum is not required, even though the occult impediment later becomes public." Accordingly, the dispensed person can lawfully and validly make use of his dispensation in the external forum after the impediment has become public.

[35] *Infra,* p. 113.
[36] *Infra,* pp. 113-114.
[37] Can. 202, § 1. Cf. also *supra,* pp. 95-97.

c) *the territoriality of the concession.* In the majority of cases dispensations are requested by and granted to individual persons on account of special causes peculiar to those individuals, as when a matrimonial impediment is removed because of the advanced age of the woman, or when the law of fast and abstinence is relaxed in someone's favor on account of bodily weakness. When the dispensation is granted in this manner, it is a personal grant and can be used wherever the dispensed person happens to be, even outside the territory of the grantor. At times, however, the use of a dispensation is restricted to the territory of the grantor, because he has, as it were, made the concession mediately by reason of the territory. Thus, when in virtue of canon 1245, § 2, an ordinary dispenses a certain place or the entire diocese from the law of fast or of abstinence or of both, those outside the designated place or, as the case may be, the diocese, cannot make use of the dispensation.[38] Finally, superiors sometimes grant a general dispensation, in such a way as to include not only all who are in their respective territories, but also all their subjects, even if they should be outside their own territory. In these cases those who are otherwise non-subjects can use the dispensation only in the territory of the one who dispenses, while subjects can use it everywhere.[39]

[38] Noldin, *De Principiis,* p. 189; Maroto, *Institutiones,* I, 367.
[39] Cappello, *Summa,* I, n. 135.

CHAPTER VIII

CAUSE FOR DISPENSATIONS

Canon 84 § 1. A lege ecclesiastica ne dispensetur sine iusta et rationabili causa, habita ratione gravitatis legis a qua dispensatur; alias dispensatio ab inferiore data illicita et invalida est.

§ 2. Dispensatio in dubio de sufficientia causae licite petitur et potest licite et valide concedi.

Article I. Kinds of Causes

The question of a just cause will be considered in the following article. But besides the just or unjust cause there are other aspects of the cause which have a bearing on dispensations.

In general, the causes which are advanced for dispensations are either final (motivating) causes or accessory causes. The former are those which of themselves are sufficient to convince the superior that a dispensation is justified. The latter, or accessory causes, are those which alone are not sufficient to induce the superior to relax the law, but which add weight to the force of the final causes.[1]

Another classification of causes is that of intrinsic and extrinsic. An intrinsic cause is one which is in direct opposition to the law. Thus, bodily weakness renders the observance of the law of fasting particularly burdensome. Or again, the fulfillment of the obligation of assisting at Mass on Sunday might stand in the way of the necessary care of the sick, which under the circumstances is to be regarded as a good to be obtained. An extrinsic cause arises from some advantage of a more general nature to be derived from the relaxation of an individual law, for example, from the fact that the authorities desire to reward the special merits of an individual or a community. It might be added that both intrinsic and extrinsic causes can be respectively either final or impulsive.

A cause, finally, is either public or private according to whether

[1] Pyrrhus, *Praxis Dispensationum,* lib. I, c. 1, n. 10.

the whole community or merely one or more individuals will benefit by the relaxation of the law in question.[2] In the early centuries of the Church the presence of a public cause was always demanded. Under the present discipline as a general rule no such insistence is made.

Article II. Just and Reasonable Cause

When the Code makes the provision that a just and reasonable cause must be present to justify the granting of a dispensation it also establishes the norm in accordance with which the justice and reasonableness of the cause is to be weighed. Not only is the one who dispenses expected to consider whether a reasonable motive is presented for departing from the common norm, but he must also weigh in the balance the cause proposed and the gravity of the law from which the dispensation is sought, to determine whether a due proportion exists between the two. There are some laws which are more closely bound up with the common good than are other laws. Others approximate the divine law. Consequently justice and reasonableness demand that a more weighty reason be present for dispensations from such laws. Thus certain causes, ordinarily regarded as sufficient—the girl's limited prospects of marriage, her advance in years beyond an age well-suited for marriage, her lack of a proper dowry, etc.—are nevertheless insufficient for a dispensation from the impediment of consanguinity in the first degree of the collateral line mixed with the second.[3]

In order that reasons for dispensations might measure up to the requirements of proportionate justice and reasonableness, it is not necessary that they be such as are sufficient to *excuse* one from the observance of a law. As Suarez[4] observes, a dispensation frow the law is not necessary if there is present a cause or a necessity which *per se* excuses one from abiding by the law. Nor need the reason be so weighty that the superior is, by relative

[2] Michiels, *Normae Generales*, II, 502, 503.

[3] Instr. S. C. Sacr., Aug. 1, 1931—*AAS.*, XXIII (1931), 413.

[4] *De legibus*, VI, c. 18, n. 14.

necessity, obliged to grant the dispensation.[5] What is required is that there be some reason which, while of itself it does not exempt from the law, is still sufficient to warrant in the prudent judgment of the superior the use of his power to make an exception in favor of one or more persons, without, however, showing any favoritism.[6] In other words, the requirements of the cause are fulfilled if in view of the particular circumstances the observance of the law would (1) constitute a proportionately grave difficulty beyond the inconvenience commonly experienced in abiding by a law, or (2) impede some reasonably proportionate benefit which would result from the relaxation of the law.

Included among the causes which are sufficient for dispensations is the special class known as *canonical causes,* that is, causes the sufficiency of which is recognized by the practice of the Roman Curia. A complete enumeration of the many causes which belong to this category cannot be made, although partial lists have been published at times. Pyrrhus,[7] for example, composed a list of fourteen such causes which were among the most widely used and accepted during his time. At a later time official lists were made by the Sacred Congregation of the Propagation of the Faith[8] and by the Apostolic Datary.[9] These last two, however, have reference only to matrimonial dispensations. It must be remembered that these enumerations of canonical causes are by no means intended to be complete lists. They are only demonstrative, since the Holy See explicitly calls them the *principal* canonical causes, indicating that there are other causes, not included in these lists,

[5] Although no one has a strict right in justice to a dispensation, at times the superior is, in a sense, obliged to grant a dispensation because of the attendant circumstances, for example, if he foresees that a grave scandal would result for the faithful from his refusal to grant a certain dispensation. Cf. Suarez, *De legibus,* VI, c. 18, n. 19-22.

[6] Suarez, *De legibus,* VI, c. 18, n. 14; Maroto, *Institutiones,* I, 365.

[7] *Praxis Disp.,* lib. I, c. 1, n. 12: personae merita, necessitas, locus, tempus, utilitas Ecclesiae, aetas, scandalum, maius bonum, futurum bonum, eventus rei, discretio, pietas, misericordia, religio. Pax Jordanus *(Elucubrationes Diversae,* lib. IX, tit. I, n. 9) lists the same causes.

[8] May 9, 1877—*Collect. S. C. de Prop. Fide,* n. 1470. *Supra,* p. 45.

[9] *ASS.,* XXXIV (1901-1902), 34-35. *Supra,* p. 46.

which are truly canonical and therefore sufficient to warrant dispensation.

Article III. Necessity of a Cause

Aside from any declaration of positive law such as that contained in canon 84, a just and reasonable cause is required for every dispensation, no matter whether it be granted by the legislator himself or by an inferior to whom dispensatory power has been communicated. This is merely a conclusion to be drawn from the application to dispensation of the principle of distributive justice, which demands of all who are placed in positions of authority that in the administration of the affairs entrusted to them they avoid favoritism. Law is an ordinance of reason, enacted for the common good, to be observed by the entire community for which it was established. If without reason this order is disrupted in favor of one or the other members of the community, an unjustified inequality is set up among the subjects of the one who relaxes the law. This in turn gives rise to the justified complaints of partiality on the part of those who without any cause of distinction are bound by the law while others are exempt.[10]

It is, of course, understood that the only cause which fulfills the requirements of justice is one which actually exists. In other words, the important question to be considered is not whether an apparently just and reasonable cause has been set forth in the petition for a dispensation. Rather, one must consider whether in reality a just reason actually exists for relaxing a law in the particular case in question. The absence of a sufficient cause, however, does not always have the same effect on a dispensation in every case.

A. Effect of the Absence of a Cause

1. Unlawfulness

The faithful administration required by Christ of those whom He places in authority to govern the Church is obligatory on all superiors alike. Accordingly, no one, not even the Roman

[10] Suarez, *De legibus*, VI, c. 18, n. 26; Cappello, *De Sacramentis*, III, 254.

Pontiff himself, can *lawfully* dispense from any law unless there is present a proportionate cause to justify his action. The arbitrary use, by a superior, of the power entrusted to him in this regard is equivalent to an abuse of his power, which, naturally, he is bound to avoid in every case.

2. *Invalidity*

Whenever an inferior grants a dispensation from a superior's law he acts necessarily by virtue of power which has been communicated to him by that superior, either directly or indirectly. But no such communication of power can be presumed to include the right to perform an unreasonable act such as the granting of a dispensation without a cause. Accordingly, an act of this kind exceeds the power with which an inferior is endowed, and as a consequence it is the same as if he did not act at all.[11] Hence there is the declaration of canon 84 that "a dispensation granted by an inferior without a just and reasonable cause is invalid." The only exception to this general rule would be a case in which the legislator has made an express provision to the contrary. The legislator can make such a provision because, just as he himself can validly dispense in the absence of a cause, so he can also grant the same power to others.[12] This type of grant, however, can in no way be presumed. On the contrary, the presumption is in favor of its absence.

Canon 1054 states that even if the only cause alleged in the petition for a dispensation from a minor matrimonial impediment is false, the dispensation is not thereby nullified. The provision of this canon must not be confused with a communication of power whereby an inferior can validly dispense without a cause. In canon 1054 the legislator does not bestow the faculty arbitrarily to grant dispensations from these impediments. The provision of this canon implies merely that if a dispensation of this kind is granted while the one who grants it is laboring under the false opinion that a cause is actually present, the dispensation nevertheless is valid.

[11] Can. 203, § 1.

[12] A Coronata, *Institutiones* I, n. 115 ad 3°.

When the legislator himself (or his successor or superior) grants a dispensation it will be valid if he has the specific intention to dispense regardless of whether or not there is a just cause for relaxing the law. If on the contrary his will to dispense is conditioned upon the existence of a just cause, and *de facto* no just cause exists, the dispensation will be invalid.

In the first supposition the validity must be admitted for the following reason. The entire obligatory force of any law depends on the will of the legislator. His will is a cause; the obligation binding his subjects to conform themselves to a certain course of action is the effect of that cause. In other words, any individual member of the community is obliged to abide by the prescriptions of the law only because the legislator wills that that individual should be so obliged. If the legislator dispenses one or the other member of the community, it is equivalent to his saying, "I no longer will that this person should be bound by the law." The relaxation of the law in that person's regard immediately becomes effective, because with the cessation of the cause (the legislator's will to oblige) the effect (that is, the obligation) also ceases.[13]

The second supposition is likewise certain. A conditioned willingness is ineffectual if the condition on which it rests is unfulfilled. In other words, when a legislator wills to dispense provided that a just cause exists, then, as a matter of fact, if a just cause is lacking, there is wanting also the intention to dispense. And when the intention to dispense is not present no relaxation of law is effected.

In trying to ascertain the validity or invalidity of a legislator's dispensation in the absence of a just cause some difficulty will be encountered if there is no direct evidence to show what was the precise intention of the legislator when he granted the dispensation. Naturally, the difficulty will vanish if there is evidence to show definitely that the legislator specifically willed to relax his law regardless of the actual existence or non-existence of a just cause, or that his will to dispense was conditioned on the

[13] Suarez, *De legibus,* VI, 19, n. 8; Benedictus XIV, *De Synodo Dioecesana,* XIII, c. 5, n. 7.

existence of such a cause. When, for example, the Roman Pontiff dispenses a couple from the matrimonial impediment of disparity of worship because of the alleged danger of their entering a civil marriage, is the dispensation valid, if as a matter of fact the danger does not exist and if, at the same time, the Pope in granting the dispensation makes no explicit mention of the actual existence of the cause, but on the strength of the alleged cause simply says that the dispensation is granted?

Authors in general would say it is valid, because they make no distinction when proposing the doctrine with respect to a legislator's dispensation in the absence of a just cause. They say simply that, although it is illicit, such a dispensation granted by the legislator is *per se* valid.[14] They evidently presume that the legislator specifically intends to dispense even though a just cause is lacking.

However, it would seem that the presumption should be in favor of the legislator's unwillingness to dispense unless a just cause exists. It seems reasonable to presume that, in line with the just and prudent administration which is entrusted to him, a legislator intends to release from the obligation of his law only those whose release is justified by a cause which really exists. In other words, the presumption is that the prevailing intention of the legislator is to dispense only if there is a just cause. So that if the only cause alleged is false, the intention to dispense is lacking and consequently the dispensation is not granted.

A summary of the foregoing opinion might be stated as follows: Even in the case of a legislator's dispensation from his own law, the dispensation is presumed to be invalid—not from lack of power but from lack of intention on the legislator's part—if there is no just cause for the dispensation. Naturally, since this is merely a presumption, it will give way to the contrary if there is evidence to support the opposite opinion. Thus, from canon 1054 it is clear that the legislator's dispensation from minor matrimonial impediments is not conditioned upon the actual existence of a just

[14] Cappello, *Summa,* I, n. 132 ad 2; Toso, *Commentaria Minora* p. 183; Chelodi, *Ius de Personis,* n. 88; Michiels, *Normae Generales* II, 501.

cause. Similarly, if it is evident that, at the time when the dispensation was granted, the legislator was aware of the absence of a just cause and if, in spite of this knowledge, he granted the dispensation, that too would prove sufficiently that his will was not conditioned on the existence of a just cause. It is unnecessary and impossible to list all the cases in which the presumption would yield to truth. Suffice it to say that it will give way in the presence of any reasonable evidence to the contrary. In the majority of cases the intention of the legislator will be quite evident, because in most cases a dispensation is granted through a rescript; and every rescript is conditioned upon the truth of the petition.[15] Consequently, with respect to the present matter of a just cause, if the only cause alleged is false—and therefore non-existent—a rescript which conveys a dispensation is invalid, unless it is a dispensation from a minor matrimonial impediment.[16]

Article IV. Causal Doubts

In the second paragraph of canon 84 the legislator makes wise provision for those cases in which there exists a doubt concerning the sufficiency of the cause. Presupposing, of course, the necessary dispensatory *power,* he provides that in a doubt of this kind a dispensation "can be both lawfully requested and lawfully and validly granted." This canon takes into consideration only the case in which a cause exists, but in which there is doubt that it is sufficient to warrant the desired dispensation. It is not concerned with a doubt concerning the existence of a cause. There is a difference between these two cases of doubt, although some authors[17] maintain that no real difference exists.

In the first case—when there is doubt concerning the sufficiency of the cause—a cause definitely exists, and by reason of canon 84, § 2, the supreme legislator supplies for the insufficiency, if in fact the existing cause really is insufficient. If actually the

[15] Can. 40.

[16] Can. 1054.

[17] A Coronata, *Institutiones,* I, n. 115; Michiels, *Normae Generales,* II, 511.

cause is sufficient, there is no need for him to supply for a deficiency, since the dispensation is valid. If, on the contrary, the cause is insufficient, the provision of this canon amounts to a delegated faculty to dispense without a *proportionate* cause, thereby rendering valid the dispensation which would otherwise be invalid. Accordingly, when a dispensation is granted under such circumstances there can no question about its validity, if it is later discovered that in reality the proposed cause was insufficient to warrant the dispensation.

In the other case, when the *existence* of a cause is doubted, it would seem at first sight that no provision is made whereby an inferior might grant a dispensation. Were he to act in such a doubt he would be running the risk of granting an invalid dispensation, since in the supposition it is possible (if not probable) that no just cause exists. He can not invoke paragraph 2 of canon 84, since this refers to something different. But, if he cannot resolve his doubt, he can regard the questionable existence of a cause as a doubt of fact and grant a valid dispensation on the strength of canon 15, which empowers ordinaries in a doubt of fact to relax any law which the Roman Pontiff is wont to relax.[18]

It will perhaps be beneficial briefly to set forth a few practical conclusions, drawn from the foregoing principles, which can serve as norms in determining the lawfulness (or unlawfulness) and validity (or invalidity) of dispensations in so far as the cause affects the same. It is, of course, understood that any reference to a dispensation granted by an inferior presupposes that he is endowed with the power to dispense.

1. If a just cause actually exists and its existence is known, a subject can lawfully request a dispensation and the legislator or an inferior can lawfully and validly grant the same. In such a case the requirements of law concerning the cause are fulfilled.

2. If a just cause actually exists but its existence is unknown to the one dispensing, the dispensation is unlawful but valid. The act of the one dispensing is unlawful since he makes an exception without being conscious of any justification for his act. But

[18] Cappello, *Summa,* I, n. 133 ad 10.

the dispensation is valid whether it is granted by the legislator or by an inferior. For in this case, the legislator's intention is evidently to dispense regardless of the absence of a just cause—which condition (i.e., the absence of a just cause) he erroneously thinks exists;[19] and with respect to an inferior's dispensation, the validity depends not on his knowledge of the cause, but on the actual existence of a just cause.[20]

It must, however, be remembered, with respect both to this case and to the following two sets of circumstances, that when a dispensation is granted by means of a rescript it is required for validity that at least one of the alleged final causes be true,[21] unless there is question of a dispensation from a matrimonial impediment of a minor degree.[22]

3. If a just cause does not exist, and its non-existence is known, the dispensation will be:

a. unlawful, since it constitutes the positing of an unreasonable act on the part of the grantor.

b. valid, if the legislator dispenses, since he does not need a just cause for the valid relaxation of his law. Moreover, the circumstances give evidence of his intention to dispense despite the absence of a just cause.[23]

c. invalid, if an inferior dispenses, unless from the express provision of the legislator the validity of the dispensation in question does not depend on the existence of a cause—for example, a dispensation from minor matrimonial impediments. Paragraph 1 of canon 84 proves this conclusively when it states that a dispensation granted by an inferior is invalid if it is granted without a just and proportionate cause.[24]

4. If a just cause does not exist but one is erroneously thought to exist:

a. an inferior's dispensation is invalid, since his power to dis-

[19] *Supra*, pp. 111-112.
[20] Can. 84, § 1. Cf. *infra*, p. 117.
[21] Can. 42, § 2.
[22] Can. 1054.
[23] *Supra*, pp. 111-112.
[24] *Supra*, p. 110.

pense extends only to those cases in which there exists a just cause for him to exercise his power. The present case is beyond the limits of his power.[25]

b. the legislator's dispensation is presumed to be invalid because of the lack of intention to dispense.[26] Under the circumstances, it seems that the legislator's intention is to dispense only for a just cause, which he erroneously thinks actually exists. In other words, working on the presumption that he intends to dispense only if a cause really exists, we can say that since the cause does not exist he does not truly intend to dispense. Of course, if there is evidence to prove the opposite intention—to dispense regardless of the absence of a cause—this presumption does not stand and the dispensation must be regarded as valid.

5. If the sufficiency of a cause is doubtful a dispensation can lawfully and validly be granted on the strength of that cause.[27] If the existence of the cause is doubtful the dispensation can lawfully and validly be granted if it is one which the Holy See is wont to grant.[28]

Article V. Knowledge and Examination of the Cause

Besides the existence of a just cause there is, moreover, required on the part of the one dispensing a knowledge of such a cause. The Council of Trent,[29] when it was prescribing the conditions under which dispensations could be granted, explicitly set forth the requirement of knowledge of the cause. And all authors[30] who consider the question also place it among the requisites at least for the lawfulness of a dispensation. It is only just that a superior, when he is relaxing a law, should know the cause for which the dispensation is granted. Otherwise his act would be an arbitrary use of his power, which cannot be justified.

[25] Cf. Can. 84. § 1; Vermeersch-Creusen, *Epitome*, I, n. 167 ad 3.

[26] *Supra*, pp. 111-112.

[27] Can. 84, § 2.

[28] Can. 15. *Supra*, p. 114.

[29] Sess. XXV, *de ref.*, c. 18—Mansi, XXXIII, 192.

[30] V.g., Suarez, *De legibus*, VI, 19, n. 2; Wernz, *Jus Decretalium*, I, n. 124; A Coronata, *Institutiones*, I, n. 115; Cicognani-O'Hara-Brennan, *Canon Law*, p. 852; Michiels, *Normae Generales*, II, 507-508.

At the same time, authors in general[31] agree that the validity of the dispensation does not depend on the knowledge of the cause, whether the one dispensing is the legislator or an inferior. As regards the legislator's relaxation of a law it is evident that if he can validly relax a law without a just cause[32] he certainly can dispense validly without the knowledge of a cause. With respect to an inferior's dispensation it can be said that such a relaxation of law is likewise valid, even in the absence of a knolwedge of the cause, because canon 84 conditions the validity of an inferior's dispensation on the *existence* of a just cause, and not on his knowledge of the same. The absence of such knowledge will render an inferior's dispensation invalid only if the superior, when he communicates the power to the inferior, establishes the knowledge of the cause as an essential condition. It is self evident that if a condition of this kind is made and it is unfulfilled the power to dispense is lacking.

One who grants a dispensation will derive the necessary knowledge of a cause through an examination of each case for which a dispensation is requested. This does not mean, however, that he must personally ascertain the existence of a just cause. This can be done by others in his stead. As a matter of fact, in the modern practice quite generally employed, the request for a dispensation is made to the ordinary by the pastor (or another priest) of the subject who desires to obtain the dispensation; and the ordinary leaves the examination of the cause of the pastor. Where this practice is followed the obligation rests on the pastor to determine as far as he is able whether a just cause exists for relaxing the law in his subject's favor.

[31] V. g., A Coronata, *Institutiones*, I, n. 115; Michiels, *Normae Generales*, II, 507-508.

[32] *Supra*, p. 111.

CHAPTER IX

INTERPRETATION OF DISPENSATIONS

Canon 85. Strictae subest interpretationi non solum dispensatio ad normam can. 50, sed ipsamet facultas dispensandi ad certum casum concessa.

Before entering upon the commentary of canon 85 a word by way of prefatory definition of the terms "strict interpretation" and "liberal interpretation" would seem to be in order.

The first rule to be followed in determining the meaning of the words used in a dispensatory grant is that which is given in canon 49 concerning the interpretation of rescripts, namely, the words used must be understood in their proper signification and in accordance with the common usage.[1] Although the Code does not contain an explicit statement of this rule with respect to dispensation, it does indicate that this direction applies to dispensations when it prescribes that "if there is no express provision concerning some affair either in the general or in the particular law, a norm of action is to be taken from laws given in similar cases . . . "[2]

An added reason for accepting this as the first rule for the interpretation of dispensations is the reasonable presumption which can be made, namely, that the one who issues a statement or a document will endeavor to use words the proper signification of which gives expression to his will.

At times, the one rule mentioned above gives sufficient direction for interpreting dispensations, inasmuch as the words used, when they are taken in their proper signification, leave no doubt concerning the precise intention of the grantor. At other times, the precise intention of the grantor is somewhat doubtful because the words used possess several proper significations. At such times, a strict interpretation is placed upon these words if, among the various proper meanings which they have, that signification

[1] Cf. also can. 18.

[2] Can. 20.

is taken which grants less than do the others; and likewise among the persons to whom, or the cases and things to which, the words in their proper meaning could be extended, those only are admitted who or which can not be excluded.[3] On the contrary, a liberal interpretation is placed upon these words if that proper signification is taken which grants more than do the other meanings.

It has been implied above that there can be no question of a strict or of a liberal interpretation when the will of the grantor is clearly indicated by the words used. Consequently, any reference in the following articles to a strict or a liberal interpretation is confined to those cases in which the words leave room for reasonable doubt concerning the will of the grantor.

ARTICLE I. INTERPRETATION OF DISPENSATIONS OTHER THAN THOSE GRANTED *Motu Proprio*

Since a dispensation, at least when it is not granted *motu proprio,* is an odious departure from the common law, it should *per se* be interpreted strictly, in accordance with the legal maxim, "That which departs from the common law is to be restrained as something odious."[4] However, it is within the power of the legislator to permit a broader interpretation if he sees fit to do so.

Aside from the exception of *motu proprio* dispensations—which will be considered in the next article—it was the opinion of the majority of canonists before the Code that a strict interpretation must be employed for all dispensations.[5] There were, however, several noteworthy pre-Code canonists who maintained that an exception to this general rule should be made if the dispensation were granted to a community.[6] For such concessions these authors would permit a liberal interpretation.

[3] Toso, *Commentaria Minora,* I, 137-138.

[4] C. 1, De filiis presbyterorum et aliis illegitime natis, I, 11, in VI°. Cf. also Reg. 28, 74, R. J. in VI°.

[5] Reiffenstuel, *Jus Canonicum Universum,* lib. 1, tit. 2, n. 451; Veranus Cajetanus Felix, *Juris Canonici Universi Commentarius Paratitlaris,* in lib. III, *De praebendis et dignitatibus,* par. II, n. 4; Barbosa, *De officio et potestate episcopi,* alleg. 33, n. 7; Sanguineti, *Juris Ecclesiastici Privati Institutiones,* p. 52; Wernz, *Jus Decretalium,* I, n. 125.

[6] Suarez, *De legibus,* VIII, c. 27, n. 7, in conjunction with VI, c. 10, n.

It was indicated above that although dispensations should *per se* receive a strict interpretation it is within the legislator's power to permit a broader interpretation if he sees fit to do so. This he has apparently chosen to do in the law of the Code, inasmuch as canon 85 prescribes that dispensations are to be interpreted strictly in accordance with the norm given for rescripts in canon 50. Canon 50 legislates for rescripts the words of which are not clear. It prescribes a strict interpretation for four classes of rescripts mentioned therein, but at the same time permits the liberal interpretation of rescripts which do not belong to any one of the categories mentioned. If the word "dispensations" were substituted for the term "rescripts" which is used in canon 50, the rule to be followed would read: "In doubt, dispensations which refer to litigations, or infringe on the acquired rights of others, or grant to private individuals favors against the law, or lastly, which were obtained for the acquisition of an ecclesiastical benefice must be strictly interpreted; all others may receive a liberal interpretation."

In the majority of cases, therefore, a strict interpretation must be applied to dispensations, since most dispensations belong to that type of concession which "grants to private individuals favors against the law." There are, however, cases in which dispensations are granted not to private individuals but to a community. In such cases, the last part of canon 50 warrants the use of a liberal interpretation, provided, of course, the dispensation in question does not belong to one of the other three categories mentioned in canon 50.[7]

There are some authors who maintain, on the contrary, that in every instance a strict interpretation must be applied, because by its very nature a dispensation is an odious exception which inflicts

13. Sanchez (*De Matrimonio,* lib. VIII, disp. 1, n. 13) implied the same when he said that dispensations should be interpreted strictly if they were given to private individuals.

[7] Vermeersch-Creusen, *Epitome,* I, n. 172; Cappello, *Summa,* I, n. 136; Bouuaert-Simenon, *Manuale Juris Canonici,* I, n. 235; A Coronata, *Institutiones,* I, n. 116.

a wound upon the law.[8] This opinion, however, would seem to be incorrect in so far as it fails to provide for the exception noted above—which exception is apparently warranted by canon 50.

ARTICLE II. INTERPRETATION OF DISPENSATIONS GRANTED *Motu Proprio*

The Code makes no special regulations for interpreting dispensations which have been granted *motu proprio.* Nor does it expressly except them from the general rules for interpretation. Yet, the special nature of such grants warrants an exception, in view of the favor which the old law attached to a concession made in this manner.

A dispensation granted *motu proprio* carries with it the implication that it is given on the initiative and out of the generosity of the one who makes the concession, even when actually it has been requested by someone.[9] Because of this fact it participates more in the nature of a favorable than of an odious concession, although as a matter of fact it must, to a certain extent, be regarded as odious, since it is an exceptional departure from the law.

It has been pointed out previously that many pre-Code canonists made no exceptions from the usual rule of applying a strict interpretation to dispensations. As a consequence, however, of the recognition of the note of favor in dispensations which were granted *motu proprio* other canonists were of the opinion that this type of concession could be interpreted more liberally than others. Among this group there were some who, in proposing their opinion, qualified it and, it would seem, restricted the liberal interpretation to *motu proprio* dispensations which were granted "for the public utility." [10] The others maintained without qualification the liberal interpretation of all *motu proprio* relaxations of law.[11]

[8] Chelodi, *Ius de Personis,* n. 88; Michiels *Normae Generales,* II, 514; Cicognani-O'Hara-Brennan, *Canon Law,* p. 857.

[9] Cf. C. 23, *de praebendis et dignitatibus,* III, 4, in VI°.

[10] Sanchez, *De matrimonio,* lib. VIII, disp. 1, n. 5; Pax Jordanus, *Elucubrationes,* lib. IX, tit. 1, n. 22.

[11] De Justis, *De Dispensationibus Matrimonialibus,* lib. I, c. 2, n. 103; Pyrrhus, *Praxis Dispensationum,* lib. I, c. 5, n. 30; Suarez, *De legibus,* VIII, c. 27, n. 8, in conjunction with VI, c. 10, n. 13.

In the law itself foundation for this opinion could be found in the words of Boniface VIII, who said, that if a concession was made at the request of someone, it was fitting that it should be restricted, but if it was granted *motu proprio,* a most liberal interpretation could be made.[12]

It remains questionable whether the legislator intended to abrogate by the prescriptions of canon 85 this particular section of the old law which provided for the liberal interpretation of dispensations granted *motu proprio.* On the one hand, it is possible that he intended to include this type of concession, and hence to abrogate the old law on this point. On the other hand, since the opening words of canon 6 say that "the Code retains for the most part the discipline hitherto in force," the special exception which the old law made in favor of concessions of this kind would seem to call for an explicit abrogation of the old law in this regard—if indeed it was the intention of the legislator to abrogate it. Consequently, until it becomes certain that the legislator intended to abolish this law, it is permissible to follow the opinion which maintains the liberal interpretation of dispensations which have been granted *motu proprio.*

Article III. Interpretation of the Faculty to Dispense

Canon 85 makes explicit reference to, and prescribes a strict interpretation for, only that type of dispensatory faculty which is granted for a specified case, that is, a single case in which definite designation is made either of the person or persons to be dispensed,[13] or of the law which is to be relaxed (if the entire community is to constitute the passive subject of the dispensatory power). The strict interpretation is decreed for such a faculty, because to all intents and purposes the faculty amounts to the dispensation itself.[14] Actually, it is not the dispensation. Nor is the one who receives a faculty of this kind merely the executor of the dispensation. But the will of the legislator that a designated

[12] C. 24, *de praebendis et dignitatibus,* III, 4, in VI°.

[13] Michiels, *Normae Generales,* II, 514; Cappello, *Summa,* I, n. 136; Toso, *Commentaria Minora,* I, 184.

[14] Suarez, *De legibus,* VI, c. 17, n. 10; Wernz, *Jus Decretalium,* I, n. 125.

law might be relaxed in favor of designated individuals is so clearly defined that any interpretation other than a strict one would be a misinterpretation of the legislator's will; and the use of a faculty thus given in accordance with a broad interpretation of the same would be in excess of the power contained in the faculty.

Faculties which, on the contrary, are given in a general way can be interpreted broadly. In this category are to be placed those faculties which are granted without a definite designation of the persons in whose favor they can be employed, whether permanently or for a definite period of time, or for a specified number of cases. This first paragraph of canon 66 declares that faculties of this kind are to be reckoned among the list of privileges beyond the law. As such they are favorable grants, and receive a broad interpretation in accordance with the legal maxim: "Favors are to be enlarged." [15]

If one were to seek a further reason why the legislator provides for the broad interpretation of habitual faculties and for the strict interpretation of the faculty for a specified case, he could find it in the fact that faculties included in the former class are given directly for the common good, while the latter category is directly intended for the benefit of the individual person or persons specified in the grant.[16]

[15] Reg. 15, R. J. in VI°: "Favorabilia amplianda sunt." Cf. also can. 50, 68.

[16] Cicognani-O'Hara-Brennan, *Canon Law,* p. 858.

CHAPTER X

CESSATION OF DISPENSATIONS

Canon 86. Dispensatio quae tractum habet successivum, cessat iisdem modis quibus privilegium, necnon certa ac totali cessatione causae motivae.

It is immediately evident from the words used that canon 86 is concerned only with the type of dispensation which implies a successive recurrence of use. It makes no provision for the other kind of dispensation which, in contradistinction, might be called a "single" dispensation. The difference between the two types derives from the distinct kind of law to which they respectively apply. "Single" dispensations relax a) laws which produce a single obligation, in the sense that once this obligation is removed, it does not of itself recur, for example, a dispensation from the impediment of disparity of worship which hinders the marriage of two designated individuals, or b) for an individual instance, a law whose obligation does recur even after a dispensation has been obtained for previous occasions. The law prescribing abstinence from flesh meat on Friday is one the obligation of which is renewed each week. A single dispensation from this law would be exemplified in the case of a person who obtained a relaxation of this law for one designated Friday. A dispensation "with successive recurrence of use" is one obtained from this latter kind of law the obligation of which recurs, but it is obtained, not for an individual instance, but perpetually or over a certain period of time, or for a designated number of occasions when the obligation arises. Thus, a person might obtain a dispensation from the law of abstinence as long as he remains in a place where it is very difficult to procure fish.

The failure, however, of canon 86 to make explicit provision for the cessation of dispensations other than those with successive recurrence of use, does not mean that these other dispensations never cease. Nor, as Michiels observes,[1] does it imply that "single" dispensations cannot cease through the same causes which

[1] *Normae Generales,* II, 516.

effect the cessation of those with successive recurrence of use. Fundamentally the two types of dispensation do not differ from each other, because a dispensation from a law with recurrent obligation is, in effect, the same as the application of a "single" dispensation repeated as often as the obligation arises. In other words, it is as though a new dispensation were granted for each instance when the obligation recurs.

The legal doctrine concerning the cessation of dispensations can be set forth more concisely if a distinction is drawn between the two stages of a dispensation. The first is the condition which obtains after the dispensatory grant has been made, but before the recipient of it has put it into use. It it this stage with which canon 86 is concerned. The second stage is reached when the person dispensed actually has used his dispensation to posit an act otherwise prohibited or to omit an otherwise prescribed act. Some authors [2] distinguish three stages, and regard the two mentioned above as the second and third steps. The first stage according to their distinction is that which exists when a dispensation is granted by means of a rescript requiring execution by a third person and when, as yet, the execution has not been made. In the present matter, however, this distinction is unnecessary. Canon 38 prescribes that rescripts granting a favor which require execution are effective only from the time of the execution. Accordingly, prior to the execution of such a dispensatory rescript the dispensation itself does not exist; and if for any reason, for example, because of revocation,[3] the rescript should cease before it has been executed, this cessation could not properly be called the cessation of a dispensation.

The distinction is made between the two different situations just described because, when the second condition obtains, namely, when the dispensation has been used in the lawful performance of the act for which ultimately it was intended, there can be no question of further cessation of that dispensation. By its very nature a dispensation continues in actual existence only as long

[2] Suarez, *De legibus,* VI, c. 20, n. 2; Michiels, *Normae Generales,* II, 517.
[3] Can. 60.

as there is some reason for its existence. The use of the dispensation in the act for which it was given, so to speak, perfects it in its own order. It is a realization of the ultimate purpose of its existence in such a way that no longer is there any reason for it to exist. Hence it naturally ceases to have actual existence.[4] After its use, the only kind of existence which can be attributed to a dispensation is a virtual existence in a lasting effect—if one results—produced by the act for which the dispensation had been granted. Thus, if one who is not yet thrity years old is chosen to be a bishop and receives a dispensation from the impediment of age, as soon as he uses his dispensation to receive consecration the relaxation of the law in that case has no further actual existence. It is an accomplished past fact which, with regard to that instance, cannot be changed or affected in any way. It is true that in some instances a lasting effect—for example, in the same case, the right to celebrate pontifical ceremonies— might be lost through a lawful act of a competent superior, but such an act would in no way have any connection with the previous dispensation as such.

What has been said in the preceding paragraph applies alike to a dispensation granted for a single act and to a dispensation granted for recurrent use in so far as its purpose has been attained in an act (or in acts) performed in virture of the dispensation. Even though its application to the latter case might not be as immediately evident, it will nevertheless be apparent from a consideration of the twofold fact, namely, that a dispensation with recurrent application, is in effect, the same as a "single" dispensation repeated as often as the obligation arises, and that such a dispensation can be partly in the second stage as described above, and partly in the first. That is, in so far as on one or more occasions a dispensation of this kind has actually been used, it has become a past fact; and as far as those occasions are concerned the ultimate purpose of its existence has been realized. Consequently with respect to those occasions it must be regarded as now non-

[4] Toso, *Commentaria Minora,* I, 185; A Coronata, *Institutiones,* I, 114; Maroto, *Institutiones,* I, 366.

existent. But, in so far as there are expected to arise other occasions to which the efficacy of the grant extends, it must be considered as existing in the first condition of a concession which has not been used. As such it will fall under the rules which govern the first stage. When, therefore, in the commentary which follows, allusion is made to the cessation of a dispensation that was granted for recurrent use it is to be understood as referring to such a dispensation *only in so far as it has not yet been used.*

Cessation of dispensation in the first stage, that is, when the dispensatory grant has been completed but the dispensation has not yet been used. It is established by canon 86 that the cessation of a dispensation granted for recurrent use is brought about through the same causes which effect the cessation of a privilege,[5] as well as through the complete and certain cessation of the motive cause on account of which the dispensation was granted. This designation of the modes of cessation exhausts all the possibilities since, as will be seen presently, it includes the causes productive of cessation which are external to the dispensation itself and those which, it might be said, are inherent in the dispensation. And, inasmuch as it is an exhaustive determination, it will be advantageous, while explaining the individual modes of cessation relative to dispensations which imply recurrent use, simultaneously to inquire whether these individual causes can likewise bring about the cessation of a "single" dispensation. As a matter of fact it will be seen that the same causes are, for the most part, applicable to both types of dispensation. Consequently, in the following explanation when a general statement with no distinction is made regarding a dispensation, it is to be understood as applying to both types.

In addition to the complete and certain expiration of the motive cause of the dispensation—which mode of cessation will be treated after the others—there are the following modes of cessation to be derived from the laws on the cessation of privileges:

1. *Revocation.* Since a dispensation is merely the expression

[5] This can, of course, be correctly understood only if it is taken in the sense that the modes of cessation for privileges apply to dispensations *provided* the nature of dispensations will permit such an application.

of a competent superior's will freeing a subject from the obligation of the law, the recall, by the competent superior, of his dispensatory will deprives the dispensation of its juridic force in such a way that the subject is once more bound to abide by the obligation of the law. By the positive provision of canon 60, however, a dispensation's juridic force continues until the recipient of it has been notified of its revocation. Therefore, if between the time of the actual revocation and the subject's notification of it the subject has used the disensation it will have to be governed by the rules given above for dispensations which have already been used.

When it is said that a dispensation ceases through a competent superior's revocation, the statement is restricted to dispensations properly so called. It does not apply to those relaxations of law which are not dispensations in the strict sense of the word, such as "dispensations" from vows. Since the obligatory force of such laws arises from the previous consent of the subject and not from the will of the superior, once it has been relaxed it can revive again only from a renewed consent of the one who has been dispensed.[6]

Relative to the superior who recalls the dispensation, the statement of principle has designedly been qualified by the note of competence, because not every superior who is empowered to dispense is likewise competent lawfully and validly to revoke the dispensation. Any superior who by proper power has relaxed a law—whether it be his own, his predecessor's or an inferior's—can always validly revoke the same dispensation because the entire obligation of the law both as to its continuance and as to its relaxation is under his power. But the revocation would be unlawful if there were no cause to justify it, since it would be an unreasonable act, inasmuch as it is presumed that the dispensation itself was a reasonable concession; and it should not be withdrawn without cause. With respect to superiors who dispense by virtue of participated power a further distinction must be made. If their dispensatory act was an exercise of power which was either ordinary or delegated *ad universitatem causarum*, they can validly and law-

[6] A Coronata, *Institutiones*, I, 114, nota 3; Michiels, *Normae Generales*, II, 518, nota 3; Suarez, *De legibus*, VIII, c. 37, n. 10.

fully revoke the dispensation if a just cause is present, but their revocation would be neither valid nor lawful in the absence of such a cause, since the presumption is that the higher superior in granting such power to dispense included also the power to recall the dispensation if there was a just cause for doing so; but it is far from likely that the superior would grant the power to revoke a dispensation without cause.[7] If, on the contrary, the superior has been delegated to grant a dispensation for a single act, he cannot validly recall the granted dispensation even in the presence of a just cause, because it is in the nature of such power to become extinct with the use of it. In other words, as soon as a person has performed the office for which he has been delegated—i.e., when he has granted the dispensation—his jurisdiction over the case has come to an end.[8]

Canon 71, in conjunction with canon 60, § 2, provides for the cessation of privileges through a contrary law; but the applicability of this mode of cessation to dispensations is ruled out by the nature of dispensation. On the one hand a dispensation cannot be contained in the law itself and therefore it cannot be governed by the first part of canon 71 which states, "Privileges contained in this Code are revoked through a general law." On the other hand the prescription of canon 60 § 2,[9] cannot be applied to dispensations, because a dispensation is by nature a validly granted relaxation of the law, already established, to which it is contrary.

In the first part of canon 77 provision is made for what might be termed an implicit revocation. Substituting the word "dispensation" for "privilege," it would read, "A dispensation also ceases if with the passage of time circumstances, in the judgment

[7] Suarez *(De legibus*, VIII, c. 37, n. 15) asserts that an inferior can revoke his dispensation from a superior's law, "because, although in dispensing he takes away the law of a superior, he does so . . . under the tacit condition . . . 'unless I shall have recalled it.' "

[8] Wernz, *Jus Decretalium,* I, n. 126; A Coronata, *Institutiones,* I, n. 117; Cappello, *Summa,* I, n. 138; Michiels, *Normae Generales,* II, 519. Cf. also, Cicognani-O'Hara-Brennan, *Canon Law,* p. 859; Maroto, *Institutiones,* I, 367.

[9] "Per legem contrariam nulla rescripta revocantur, nisi aliud in ipsa lege caveatur, aut lex lata sit a Superiore ipsius rescribentis."

of the Superior, change in such a way that it has proved harmful or its use is unlawful." In such circumstances it is not necessary for the superior explicitly to revoke the dispensation. Immediately he has reasonably formed the judgment that the circumstances are such as have been set forth in canon 77, the dispensation loses its force. The superior should, however, notify the grantee that he has formed this judgment. The revocation itself really proceeds from the supreme legislator, who has included it in the law, ever if the dispensation has been granted by an inferior. However, the supreme legislator's revocation is apparently conditioned upon the presence of the superior's judgment that the required circumstances exist.[10]

The characteristic of harmfulness is present if the dispensation proves to be injurious to the public good, to third persons, and even to the recipient of the dispensation in accordance with the maxim: "That which is granted to someone as a favor ought not to be turned unto his detriment." [11] It is likewise present if the burden which it places on others is excessively increased.[12] Its use becomes unlawful when because of the changed circumstances it is contrary to natural justice or equity.

Relative to the competence of a superior to adjudge the circumstances, the Code does not explicitly determine who are qualified; but canonists agree that the judgment must be made either by the grantor himself, by his superior or by his successor. An inferior is not competent unless, of course, one of the former three has delegated him to examine the circumstances and to pass judgment on the harmfulness or unlawfulness of the further use of the dispensation.[13] But while the various local ordinaries are not empowered to pass judgment with respect to dispensations which have been granted directly by the Holy See, the vigilance

[10] Michiels, *Normae Generales,* II, 429; Cappello, *Summa,* I, n. 175.

[11] Reg. 61, R. J. in VI°.

[12] Toso, *Commentaria Minora,* I, 173; Cicognani-O'Hara-Brennan, *Canon Law,* p. 820.

[13] Toso, *Commentaria Minora,* I, 173; Vermeersch-Creusen, *Epitome,* I, n. 155; A Coronata, *Institutiones,* I. n. 106; Michiels *Normae Generales,* II, 429; Cicognani-O'Hara-Brennan, *Canon Law,* p. 820.

which is entrusted to them places them under obligation to notify the Holy See if it is brought to their attention that the use of such a dispensation has become harmful or illicit.[14]

2. *Renunciation.* A dispensation comes to an end if the person in whose favor it was granted expressly rejects it and his renunciation is accepted by a competent superior,[15] provided, of course, the dispensation is one which that individual is at liberty to renounce. A private individual may not renounce dispensations which have been granted to him by reason of his membership in a given community or his incorporation in a certain rank of honor or his constituency in a determined locality.[16] Nor may a community or a group—and much less a private individual—reject a dispensation if such rejection would be prejudicial to the Church or to other persons.[17]

For the dispensation to cease in such a way that the obligation of the law once more binds the person who had received the dispensation, the competent superior's acceptance of its renunciation is necessary. Otherwise the obligation of the law would not revive, since it can arise only from the will of the superior. The individual might reject the dispensation and, as it were, bind himself to act in accordance with the law. But until the competent superior has accepted the rejection and has thereby implicitly again included that subject under the law, the law can have no binding force over that individual. Consequently, if before the superior's acceptance of his renunciation the subject should recall the renunciation, he would still be free from the obligation of the law and could act in accordance with his dispensation.[18]

When, however, there is question of the renunciation of a "dispensation" from a law the obligation of which arises from the prior consent of the individual, the superior's acceptance of this renunciation is not necessary, for the very reason that in

[14] Cf. Can. 78.
[15] Can. 72, § 1.
[16] Can. 72, § 3.
[17] Can. 72, § 4. Cf. Maroto, *Institutiones,* I, 367.
[18] A Coronata, *Institutiones,* I, n. 117; Cappello, *Summa,* I, n. 138.

such a case the obligation of the law as incumbent upon that individual does not proceed from the superior's will.[19] The revocatory act is an implicit renewal of consent which begets an obligation similar to that which existed before the dispensation was granted.

What has been said above relative to the competence of superiors to revoke dispensations should be recalled in this connection also, namely, that a superior who has been delegated for a single act of dispensing is not competent to accept a subject's renunciation of a dispensation when granted within these limits, because his power ceases with the performance of the one act for which he has been delegated. With regard to other superiors, their competence continues.

The question of *tacit renunciation* based on the non-use or contrary usage arises with reference to dispensations, because canon 76 makes provision for the effect of non-use or contrary usage on the cessation of privileges.

The effect of the mere non-use or contrary usage on a dispensation can be determined quite easily. Since a dispensation is merely a facultative concession which juridically cannot be burdensome to others, it admits of the application of the principle which is applied in canon 76 to non-onerous privileges, namely, that they do not cease through non-use or contrary usage. Although on the one hand no explicit legislation establishes in a positive way this principle with regard to dispensations,[20] on the other hand there is no legislation which decrees that a dispensation ceases from non-use or contrary usage. Consequently, unless a special act of the superior intervenes to reestablish the obligation, the dispensation continues in force, since it is only from his will that the obligation can again arise.[21]

[19] A Coronata, *Institutiones,* I, n. 117; *Cappello,* Summa, I, n. 138; Wernz, *Jus Decretalium,* I, 126.

[20] Canon 86 does not provide precisely for this point. It does not state that a dispensation continues if a privilege would remain in force under similar circumstances. Provision is made only for the cessation of dispensations which are granted for recurrent use if a cause is present which, were it a question of a privilege, would effect the cessation of the privilege.

[21] A Coronata (*Institutiones,* I. n. 117) maintains the cessation through non-use or contrary use.

Greater difficulty, however, is encountered and less certainty results when there is question of a tacit renunciation, because of the practical impossibility of determining when such a renunciation is present. Evidently something more than the mere non-use or contrary use is required to establish the tacit rejection of a dispensation. One can easily conceive of a dispensed person who might not wish to exercise the faculty which his dispensation gives him, but who at the same time certainly has no intention of renouncing his freedom from the law. Consequently, in addition to the non-exercise of his facultative right—whether the non-exercise consists in the non-use of, or in a use that is contrary to, the dispensation—there must be other circumstances which of themselves are sufficient reasonably to lead one to the conclusion that the dispensed person really wills to renounce his dispensation.[22] The main difficulty rests precisely in this, that it is well nigh impossible to designate in practice, any set of circumstances which will certainly justify the conclusion that the *tacit* renunciation of a dispensation is present. Theoretically, it must be admitted that if there is a tacit rejection which comes to the notice of the superior and he in turn accepts it, the dispensation ceases. But when it comes down to practice the theory is of little avail, because of the difficulty of applying it with any degree of certainty.

Some authors [23] have maintained that a tacit renunciation is present if a person is in possession of a dispensation and if he obtains another dispensation which he cannot use simultaneously with the one previously obtained. This would be exemplified in the case of one who had been dispensed to marry a consanguine relative, but who did not use his dispensation and now obtains a similar dispensation to marry some other blood-relation.

According to others [24] the first dispensation is not lost in these circumstances. On the contrary, the person in question would be

[22] Toso, *Commentaria Minora,* I, 122; Michiels, *Normae Generales,* II, 413.

[23] Sanchez, *De Matrimonio,* lib. VIII, disp. 22, n. 19; Suarez, *De legibus,* VI, c. 20, n. 9.

[24] Cappello, *Summa,* I, n. 138; Michiels, *Normae Generales,* II, 521.

at liberty to use either one of the dispensations, or even to use both successively if the inconsistency between the use of the two dispensations had ceased to exist. Thus if he were to use his second dispensation to enter marriage and if later his wife were to die, he could still use the first dispensation to enter the previously contemplated marriage.[25]

In the absence of either a superior's revocation or the subject's express renunciation—whether explicit or implicit—for all practical purposes it seems that a tacit renunciation must be excluded from the causes effective to the cessation of dispensations, because of the difficulty of establishing the actual existence of such a renunciation. There would also seem to be a reasonable presumption against the existence of a tacit renunciation, namely, that the one dispensed wishes to retain whatever freedom he possesses and therefore that he desires the dispensation to continue. Moreover, as Suarez observes[26] with reference to another case, an act is not necessarily inconsistent with the dispensation itself (and therefore with the removal of an obligation) merely because of the fact that it is inconsistent with the use of that dispensation. Hence, a dispensation can continue in force even though a condition exists which prevents the use of it.

3. *Termination of grantor's authority.* In accordance with the legal maxim,[27] "It is fitting that the favor of a ruler should be permanent," it is to be expected that a dispensation granted absolutely should continue indefinitely, even though the authority of the one who granted it should end. This must, or course, be understood in the sense that if the dispensation was given for a definite case, the freedom from the obligation persists until the dispensation has been used for that case, but, if there is question of a concession, which implies recurrent use, the liberty extends to

[25] It should be noted that in such a case there is a possibility that the first marriage will give rise to the impediment of affinity with respect to the second marriage. In this event, a dispensation from the impediment of affinity would, of course, have to be obtained before one could enter the second marriage.

[26] *De Legibus,* VI, c. 20, n. 10.

[27] Reg. 16, R. J. in VI°.

all the succeeding instances of the otherwise recurrent obligation. But while it is fitting that a dispensation should be characterized by this quasi-permanence, it is within the right of the grantor to place limits upon its extension. Thus he can make the continuance of the dispensation conditional upon the perseverance of his personal pleasure by the addition of such a phrase as *ad beneplacitum nostrum.* If he places such a condition the dispensation naturally continues only as long as his will (that the dispensation should continue) lasts. And since it is only by reason of his will *as a competent superior* that the dispensation exists, it will come to an end not only by a change of will while he remains in office, but also by the termination of his authority, through any cause, which of necessity puts an end to the perseverance of his will in its capacity as the will of a superior.

In accordance with the parallel law regarding privileges[28] this is the only type of dispensation which necessarily ceases with the termination of a superior's authority, namely, one which has been given with the phrase *ad beneplacitum nostrum* or some equivalent phrase. The inclusion, however, of the phrases *ad beneplacitum Sedis, donec revocavero,* and *donec revocetur* does not place the dispensation in the same category. For in the case of the first one, even though the authority of an individual incumbent should end, the See continues. In the case of either of the other two phrases a positive revocatory act is required; and the dispensation thus granted terminates only when such an act is posited.

4. *Lapse of time or exhaustion of the number of cases.* For reasons somewhat similar to those set forth with respect to the termination of the grantor's authority, a dispensation, if it has been granted for a definite time or for a determined number of cases, ceases as soon as either the time has elapsed for which it was granted or it has been used in the specified number of cases.[29] The time-element in such a grant might be assigned as a definitely

[28] Can. 73.
[29] Can. 77.

designated number of days, months or years, or else its terminal date might be less exactly designated, although the completion of the time can otherwise be definitely determined, for example, when a law is relaxed as long as the condition of ill health continues. The precise reason on account of which a dispensation ceases in these circumstances is, of course, the fact that the grantor has limited his will to dispense. Once the limit of time or number of cases has been reached the will to dispense—and thereby also the dispensation itself—terminates.

5. *Extinction of the dispensed person.* When a dispensation is granted in a manner which corresponds, in the matter of privileges, to the concession of a *personal* privilege, the very nature of the grant demands the simultaneous cessation of the dispensation with the termination of the existence of the person who received the grant.[30] For, once the subject in whom the dispensation immediately resides ceases to exist, the dispensation itself must likewise terminate, because its foundation, as it were, is removed.[31]

These "personal" dispensations are either: (a) those granted to physical persons whether individually or commonly, that is, granted to all persons belonging to a certain state or class, for example, Cardinals, or patrons;[32] in either of which cases the dispensation ceases with the termination of the physical life of its recipient, or (b) those granted to a collegiate moral person, such as a community or a religious institute. In this case the dispensation ends with the extinction of the juridic person—which extinction is effected only if the moral person is suppressed by legitimate authority, or if it has ceased to exist over a period of one hundred years.[33]

6. When a person's association with a certain object or place is the medium through which he obtains a dispensation, the *absolute destruction of the thing or of the place* causes the cessation of the dispensation. Such a concession corresponds to a *real* privilege,[34]

[30] Can. 74.

[31] Toso, *Commentaria Minora*, I, 170.

[32] Michiels, *Normae Generales*, II, 332; Cicognani-O'Hara-Brennan, *Canon Law*, p. 782.

[33] Can. 102.

[34] Can. 75.

and is present, for example, if a dispensation is granted to the occupant of an office, not personally, but through the office, or if it is granted to the rector of a church, likewise not personally, but mediately because of his connection with that church. When the concession is made in this manner, it passes to those who successively have the same connection with the object or place through which the original recipient obtained the dispensation.[35]

7. *Certain and complete cessation of the motive cause.* Relative to the termination of a dispensation through the certain and complete cessation of the motive cause on account of which it was granted, a distinction must be drawn between "single" dispensations and such as admit of recurrent use. It is definitely established that a dispensation which admits of recurrent use loses its jurdic force as soon as its motive cause has unquestionably and completely ceased.[36] It is, on the contrary, by far the more common opinion that a "single" dispensation does not end even though the motive cause should thus cease before the dispensation has been used, unless, of course, the dispensation has been granted conditionally upon the perseverance of the motive cause.[37]

Aside from the fact that the Code expressly provides for the termination, in these circumstances, of dispensations which are granted for recurrent use, while it prescribes nothing in this regard about "single" dispensations, a reason for the different doctrines can be found in the different nature of the two types of relaxation. Of the nature of the former Suarez says in substance that a law whose obligation recurs at regular intervals is virtually a multiple law and imposes, as it were, a new obligation in each recurrent instance. In a similar way a dispensation from such a law is virtually multiple, with the result that all the recurrent obligations are not simultaneously removed, but

[35] Noldin, *De Principiis Theologiae Moralis* (18. ed., Oeniponte: Rauch, 1925), p. 188.

[36] Can. 86.

[37] Suarez, *De legibus*, VI, c. 20, n. 15; Wernz, *Jus Decretalium*, I, n. 126; Cappello, *Summa*, I, n. 137; Cicognani-O'Hara-Brennan, *Canon Law*, p. 859; Michiels, *Normae Generales*, II, 523; A Coronata, *Institutiones*, I, n. 117.

individual dispensations, so to speak, are granted for the individual cases of recurrence and each requires its own cause. Thus, with respect to the Lenten fast "although a dispensation from it seems to be given for the entire Lenten period, it is not given in such a way that immediately the complete bond for the whole of Lent is removed, but that successively it is removed as it successively obliges, if the same reason for excuse perseveres."[38] Consequently, as long as there remain possible recurrent obligations to which the dispensation, as granted, could naturally extend, the immediate effect of the dispensation—the relaxation of a law —is not completely realized. On the contrary, a "single" dispensation granted absolutely wholly achieves its immediate effect as soon as it is granted, because the complete bond of the law is entirely removed, and hence can be restored only by an act of the superior's will.

Another possible explanation, likewise drawn from the nature of the grant, is the following. The prescriptions of can. 86 clearly show that it is the will of the supreme legislator that any dispensation which implies a recurrent use is granted provisionally upon the continuance of the motivating cause. Contrariwise, when there is question of a "single" dispensation, although it is within the grantor's power to make his concession provisional upon the perseverance of the cause until the dispensation is actually used for the purpose for which it was obtained, there is no such expression of the legislator's will to the effect that all "single" dispensations are thus conditioned. Accordingly, in the absence of an expression of the grantor's will to the contrary, such a relaxation of law does not depend on the continued existence of the motivating cause, especially since a dispensation of this kind is, as it were, perfected immediately in the relaxation of the law.

[38] Suarez, *De legibus,* VI, c. 20, n. 18.

PARTICULAR CONCLUSIONS

1. Although, in accordance with the strict interpretation which must be placed on canon 43, the terms of this canon do not invalidate the granting of a dispensation by one of the Roman Congregations or Offices, when such a concession is made subsequently to the Roman Pontiff's refusal of the same dispensation, the invalidity of the grant must be admitted in accordance with other principles of law.

2. If a local ordinary uses the power granted by canon 81 when an emergency arises after he has already instituted recourse to the Holy See, the dispensation is valid, even though it should later be learned, upon receipt of the Holy See's reply, that the petition had already been refused at the moment when the local ordinary performed the dispensatory act.

3. The broad interpretation of the last part of canon 81—so as to include urgent cases which involve matrimonial dispensations—would not have forestalled the possibility of a practical advantage to be gained from the special concession made in the Decree *Proxima Sacra,* issued by the Sacred Consistorial Congregation, April 25, 1918.

4. Even in the case of a legislator's dispensation from his own law, the dispensation is *presumed* to be invalid, whenever there is no just cause present for the dispensation—not, however, from lack of power, but, rather, from lack of intention on the legislator's part

BIBLIOGRAPHY

Sources

Acta Apostolicae Sedis, Commentarium Officiale, Romae, 1909-

Acta Sanctae Sedis, 41 vols., Romae, 1865-1908.

Codex Iuris Canonici, Pii X Pontificis Maximi iussu digestus Benedicti XV auctoritate promulgatus, Romae: Typis Polyglottis Vaticanis, 1917.

Codicis Iuris Canonici Fontes cura Emi Petri Card. Gasparri editi, 8 vols., Romae: Typis Polyglottis Vaticanis, 1923-1938. (Vols. VII-VIII ed. *cura et studio Emi Iustiniani Card. Serédi.*)

Collectanea S. Congregationis de Propaganda Fide, 2 vols., Romae: Typographia Polyglotta S. C. de Propaganda Fide, 1907.

Corpus Iuris Canonici, ed. Richter-Friedberg, 2 vols., Lipsiae, 1881.

Decretales D. Gregorii Papae IX suae integritati una cum glossis restitutae, Romae: in Aedibus Populi Romani, 1582.

Decretum Gratiani, emendatum et notationibus illustratum una cum glossis Gregorii XIII Pont. Max. iussu editum, 2 vols., Romae: in Aedibus Populi Romani, 1582.

Enchiridion Symbolorum Definitionum et Declarationum de rebus fidei et morum, ed. Denzinger, H-Bannwart, C., 10 ed., Friburgi Brisgoviae: Herder, 1908.

Liber Sextus Decretalium D. Bonifacii Papae VIII suae integritati una cum Clementinis et Extravagantibus, earumque glossis restitutus, Romae: in Aedibus Populi Romani, 1582.

Mansi, J., *Sacrorum Conciliorum Nova et Amplissima Collectio,* 53 vols., Parisiis, 1901-1927.

Migne, J. P., *Patrologiae Cursus Completus, Series Graeca,* 161 vols., Parisiis, 1856-1866.

——— *Patrologiae Cursus Completus, Series Latina,* 221 vols, Parisiis, 1844-1864.

Monumenta Germaniae Historica, Libelli de Lite, edidit Societas Aperiendis Fontibus Rerum Germanicarum Medii Aevi, Hannoverae, 1891-1892.

Pallottini, Salvator, *Collectio Omnium Conclusionum et Resolutionum Congregationis Concilii ab anno 1564-1860,* 17 vols., Romae, 1868-1893.

Thesaurus Resolutionum Sacrae Congregationis Concilii, 167 vols., Romae, 1718-1908.

Authors

Alphonsus de Ligorio, *Theologia Moralis,* nova ed., Vol. I, Vesuntione, 1828.

[Bachofen], Charles Augustine, *A Commentary on the New Code of Canon Law,* 4. ed., 8 vols., St. Louis: B. Herder, 1921-1929.

Baldus de Ubaldis, *In Decretalium Volumen Commentaria.* Venetiis, 1580.

Barbosa, A., *De officio et Potestate Episcopi,* Lugduni, 1658.

——— *Summa Apostolicarum Decisionum,* Lugduni, 1658.

Benedictus XIV, *De Synodo Dioecesana,* 3 vols., Romae, 1783.

Blat, Albertus, *Commentarium Textus Codicis Iuris Canonici,* 6 vols., Romae: in Instituto Pii IX, 1921-1927.

Bouix, Dominique, *Tractatus de Episcopo,* 2 vols., Paris, 1859.

Bouscaren, T. Lincoln, *The Canon Law Digest,* Milwaukee: Bruce, 1934 (Vol. I), 1937 (Vol. II), 1938 (Supplement).

Bouuaert, F. C.-Simenon, G., *Manuale Juris Canonici,* 3. ed., 3 vols., Gandae et Leodii, 1930.

Brys, J., *De Dispensatione in Iure Canonico,* Brugis: Beyaert, 1925.

Cappello, Felix M., *Summa Iuris Canonici,* 2. ed., 3 vols., Romae: apud Aedes Universitatis Gregorianae, 1932-1936.

——— *Tractatus Canonico-Moralis De Sacramentis,* 2 ed., Vol., III, Romae: Marietti, 1927.

Chelodi, Joannes, *Ius de Personis,* Tridenti: Libr. Edit. Tridentum, 1922.

Cicognani, A.-O'Hara, J.-Brennan, F., *Canon Law,* 2 ed., Philadelphia: The Dolphin Press, 1935.

Coronata, Matthaeus Conte a, *Institutiones Iuris Canonici,* Vol. I, Taurini: Marietti, 1928.

D'Annibale, J., *Summula Theologiae Moralis,* 3. ed., 3 vols., Romae: A. Saraceni, 1891.

De Justis, Vincentius, *De Dispensationibus Matrimonialibus Tractatus,* Lucae, 1726.

De Marca, P., *De Concordia Sacerdotii et Imperii seu de Libertatibus Ecclesiae Gallicanae,* 3 vols., Neapoli, 1771.

Durandus, G., *Speculum Iuris,* 2. ed., Brugis: Societas Sancti Augustini, 1577.

Esmein, A., *Le Mariage en Droit Canonique,* 2. ed., 2 vols., Paris: Libr. de Recueil Sirey, 1929-1935.

Farrugia, P. Nicolaus, *De Matrimonio et Causis Matrimonialibus,* Taurini-Romae: Marietti, 1924.

Febronius, J., *De Statu Ecclesiae et Legitima Potestate Romani Pontificis,* Bouillon, 1764.

Gasparri, Petrus, *Tractatus Canonicus de Matrimonio,* ed. nova ad mentem Codicis Iuris Canonici, Romae: Typis Polyglottis Vaticanis, 1932.

Guilfoyle, Merlin, *Custom,* The Catholic University of America, Canon Law Studies, n. 105, Washington: The Catholic University of America, 1937.

Hefele, C., *Histoire des Conciles.* Nouvelle Traduction Francaise par Dom. H. Leclercq, Paris, 1907-1931.

Hostiensis (Henry of Susa), *In Quinque Decretalium Libros Commentaria,* Venetiis, 1581.

——— *Summa Aurea,* Venetiis, 1570.

Hughes, P., *A History of the Church,* New York: Sheed and Ward, 1935.
Innocentius IV, *In Quinque Libros Decretalium Necnon In Decretales Per Eumdem Editas Commentaria Doctissima,* Venetiis, 1578.
Jordanus, Pax, *Elucubrationes Diversae,* 3 vols., Coloniae Allobrogum et Lugduni, 1729.
Kirch, C., *Enchiridion Fontium Historiae Ecclesiasticae Antiquae,* Friburgi Brisgoviae, 1923.
Laspeyres, E., *Bernardi Papiensis summa Decretalium,* Ratisbonae, 1860.
Michiels, P. G., *Normae Generales Juris Canonici,* 2 vols., Lublin, Polonia: Universitas Catholica, 1929.
Maroto, P., *Institutiones Iuris Canonici,* 3 ed., Vol. I, Romae: Commentarium pro Religiosis, 1921.
Noldin, H., *De Principiis Theologiae Moralis,* 18 ed., Oeniponte: Rauch, 1925.
Ojetti, Benedictus, *Commentarium in Codicem Iuris Canonici,* Vol. I, Romae: apud Aedes Universitatis Gregoraniae, 1927.
——— *Synopsis Rerum Moralium et Iuris Pontificii,* Romae, 1899.
O'Mara, W., *Canonical Causes for Matrimonial Dispensations,* The Catholic University of America, Canon Law Studies, n. 96, Washington: The Catholic University of America, 1935.
Panormitanus Abbas (Nicolaus de Tudeschis), *Commentaria,* 8 vols., Venetiis, 1588.
Pirhing, Ernricus, *Ius Canonicum in V Libros Decretalium Distributum,* Venetiis, 1759.
Pyrrhus, Corradus, *Praxis Dispensationum Apostolicarum,* Neapoli, 1641.
Raymundus de Pennafort, *Summa,* Veronae, 1744.
Reiffenstuel, A., *Ius Canonicum Universum,* 4 vols., Romae, 1843-1844.
Reimarus, T., *Petri Blessensis opusculum de distinctionibus in canonum interpretatione adhibendis sive Speculum Iuris Canonici,* Berolini, 1857.
Sanchez, Thomas, *De Sancto Matrimonii Sacramento Disputationum tomi tres,* Lugduni, 1669.
Sanguineti, Sebastianus, *Iuris Ecclesiastici Privati Institutiones,* Romae, 1884.
Schmalzgrueber, Franciscus, *Ius Canonicum Universum,* 12 vols., Romae, 1843-1845.
Singer, H., *Die Summa Decretorum des Magister Rufinus,* Paderborn, 1902.
Stiegler, M. A., *Dispensation, Dispensationswesen und Dispensationsrecht im Kirchenrecht,* Mainz, 1901.
Suarez, Franciscus, *Opera Omnia,* nova ed., 26 vols., Parisiis, 1856-1861.
Thaner, F., *Anselmi Collectio Canonum, una cum Collectione Minore,* Innsbruck, 1906 (Fasc. I), 1915 (Fasc. II).

Thiel, A., *Epistolae Romanorum Pontificum Genuinae,* Vol. I, Brunsbergae, 1868.

Thomas Aquinas, *Quaestiones Disputatae et Quaestiones Duodecim Quodlibetales,* (Vol. V, *Quaestiones Quodlibetales),* Taurini-Romae: Marietti, 1931.

——— *Summa Theologica,* 6 vols., Parisiis: Vivès, 1895.

Thomassinus, L., *Vetus et Nova Ecclesiae Disciplinia,* 3 vols., Venetiis, 1730.

Toso, Albertus, *Ad Codicem Juris Canonici Commentaria Minora,* 2. ed., Vol. I, Romae: ex officina Typographica Vinciana, 1921.

Van Hove, A., *De Legibus Ecclesiasticis,* Mechliniae-Romae: Dessain, 1930.

Veranus, Cajetanus Felix, *Juris Canonici Universi Commentarius Paratitlaris,* 3 vols., Monachii, 1703.

Vermeersch, A.-Creusen, J., *Epitome Iuris Canonici,* 3. ed., 3 vols., Mechliniae-Romae: Dessain, 1927.

Wernz, Franciscus, *Ius Decretalium,* 2. ed., 6 vols., Romae, 1906.

Wernz, F.-Vidal, P., *Ius Canonicum,* Vol. V, Romae: apud Aeaes Universitatis Gregorianae, 1925.

Zittelli, Z., *Apparatus Iuris Ecclesiastici,* Romae: ex Typis Soc. Edit. Rom., 1886.

Periodicals

Appollinaris, Commentarium Iuridico-Canonicum, Romae, 1928-

Collationes Brugenses, Brugis, 1896-

Ephemerides Theologicae Lovanienses, Louvain, 1924-

BIOGRAPHICAL NOTE

Edward Michael Reilly was born September 15, 1911, at Pottsville, Pennsylvania. After completing his grammar school education in St. Patrick's School in the same city, he entered Pottsville Catholic High School. In 1927 he entered St. Charles Seminary, Overbrook, Pennsylvania, where he received the degree of Bachelor of Arts in 1933. He was ordained to the priesthood at Philadelphia, Pennsylvania, May 30, 1936. In September of the same year he entered the Catholic University of America to pursue a course of studies in the School of Canon Law. In June, 1937, he received the degree of Bachelor of Canon Law. In the same month of the following year he received the Licentiate in Canon Law.

ALPHABETICAL INDEX

CANON LAW STUDIES

1. Freriks, Rev. Celestine A., C.PP.S., J.C.D., Religious Congregations in Their External Relations, 121 pp., 1916.
2. Galliher, Rev. Daniel M., O.P., J.C.D., Canonical Elections, 117 pp., 1917.
3. Borkowski, Rev. Aurelius L., O.F.M., J.C.D., De Confraternitatibus Ecclesiasticis, 136 pp., 1918.
4. Castillo, Rev. Cayo, J.C.D., Disertacion Historico-Canonica sobre la Potestad del Cabildo en Sede Vacante o Impedida del Vicario Capitular, 99 pp., 1919 (1918).
5. Kubelbeck, Rev. William J., S.T.B., J.C.D., The Sacred Pentitentiaria and Its Relations to Faculties of Ordinaries and Priests, 129 pp., 1918.
6. Petrovits, Rev. Joseph J.C., S.T.D., J.C.D., The New Church Law On Matrimony, X-461 pp., 1919.
7. Hickey, Rev. John J., S.T.B., J.C.D., Irregularities and Simple Impediments in the New Code of Canon Law, 100 pp., 120.
8. Klekotka, Rev. Peter J., S.T.B., J.C.D., Diocesan Consultors, 179 pp., 1920.
9. Wanenmacher, Rev. Francis, J.C.D., The Evidence in Ecclesiastical Procedure Affecting the Marriage Bond, 1920 (Printed 1935).
10. Golden, Rev. Henry Francis, J.C.D., Parochial Benefices in the New Code, IV-119 pp., 1921 (Printed 1925).
11. Koudelka, Rev. Charles J., J.C.D., Pastors, Their Rights and Duties According to the New Code of Canon Law, 211 pp., 1921.
12. Melo, Rev. Antonius, O.F.M., J.C.D., De Exemptione Regularium, X-188 pp., 1921.
13. Schaaf, Rev. Valentine Theodore, O.F.M., S.T.B., J.C.D., The Cloister, X-180 pp., 1921.
14. Burke, Rev. Thomas Joseph, S.T.D., J.C.D., Competence in Ecclesiastical Tribunals, IV-117 pp., 1922.
15. Leech, Rev. George Leo, J.C.D., A Comparative Study of the Constitution, "Apostolicae Sedis" and the "Codex Iuris Canonici," 179 pp., 1922.
16. Motry, Rev. Hubert Louis, S.T.D., J.C.D., Diocesan Faculties According to the Code of Canon Law, II-167 pp., 1922.
17. Murphy, Rev. George Lawrence, J.C.D., Delinquencies and Penalties in the Administration and Reception of the Sacraments, IV-121 pp., 1923.
18. O'Reilly, Rev. John Anthony, S.T.B., J.C.D., Ecclesiastical Sepulture in the New Code of Canon Law, II-129 pp., 1923.

19. Michalicka, Rev. Wenceslas Cyrill, O.S.B., J.C.D., Judicial Procedure in Dismissal of Clerical Exempt Religious, 107 pp., 1923.
20. Dargin, Rev. Edward Vincent, S.T.B., J.C.D., Reserved Cases According to the Code of Canon Law, IV-103, pp., 1924.
21. Godfrey, Rev. John A., S.T.B., J.C.D., The Right of Patronage According to the Code of Canon Law, 153 pp., 1924.
22. Hagedorn, Rev. Francis Edward, J.C.D., General Legislation on Indulgences, II-154 pp., 1924.
23. King, Rev. James Ignatius, J.C.D., The Administration of the Sacraments to Dying Non-Catholics, V-141 pp., 1924.
24. Winslow, Rev. Francis Joseph, A.F.M., J.C.D., Vicars and Prefects Apostolic, IV-149 pp., 1924.
25. Correa, Rev. Jose Servelion, S.T.L., J.C.D., La Potestad Legislativa de la Iglesia Catolica, IV-127 pp., 1925.
26. Dugan, Rev. Henry Francis, A.M., J.C.D., The Judiciary Department of the Diocesan Curia, 87 pp., 1925.
27. Keller, Rev. Charles Frederick, S.T.B., J.C.D., Mass Stipends, 167 pp., 1925.
28. Paschang, Rev. John Linus, J.C.D., The Sacramentals According to the Code of Canon Law, 129 pp., 1925.
29. Pointek, Rev. Cyrillus, O.F.M., S.T.B., J.C.D., De Indulto Exclaustrationis necnon Saecularizationis, XIII-289 pp., 1925.
30. Kearney, Rev. Richard Joseph, S.T.B., J.C.D., Sponsors at Baptism According to the Code of Canon Law, IV-127 pp., 1925.
31. Bartlett, Rev. Chester Joseph, A.M., LL.B., J.C.D., The Tenure of Parochial Property in the United States of America, V-108 pp., 1926.
32. Kilker, Rev. Adrian Jerome, J.C.D., Extreme Unction, V-425 pp., 1926.
33. McCormick, Rev. Robert Emmett, J.C.D., Confessors of Religious, VIII-266 pp., 1926.
34. Miller, Rev. Newton Thomas, J.C.D., Founded Masses According to the Code of Canon Law, VII-93 pp., 1926.
35. Roelker, Rev. Edward G., S.T.D., J.C.D., Principles of Privilege According to the Code of Canon Law, XI-166 pp., 1926.
36. Bakalarczyk, Rev. Richardus, M.I.C., J.U.D., De Novitiatu, VIII-208 pp., 1927.
37. Pizzuti, Rev. Lawrence, O.F.M., J.U.L., De Parochis Religiosis, 1927. (Not printed).
38. Bliley, Rev. Nicholas Martin, O.S.B., J.C.D., Altars According to the Code of Canon Law, XIX-132 pp., 1927.
39. Brown, Mr. Brendan Francis, A.B. LL.M., J.U.D., The Canonical Juristic Personality with Special Reference to Its Status in the United States of America, V-212 pp., 1927.

40. Cavanaugh, Rev. William Thomas, C.P., J.U.D., The Reservation of the Blessed Sacrament, VIII-101 pp., 1927.
41. Doheny, Rev. William J., C.S.C., A.B., J.U.D., Church Property: Modes of Acquisition, X-118 pp., 1927.
42. Feldhaus, Rev. Aloysius H., C.PP.S., J.C.D., Oratories, IX-141 pp., 1927.
43. Kelly, Rev. James Patrick, A.B., J.C.D., The Jurisdiction of the Simple Confessor, X-208 pp., 1927.
44. Neuberger, Rev. Nicholas J., J.C.D., Canon 6 or the Relation of the Codex Juris Canonici to the Preceding Legislation, V-95 pp., 1927.
45. O'Keefe, Rev. Gerald Michael, J.C.D., Matrimonial Dispensations, Powers of Bishops, Priests and Confessors, VIII-232 pp., 1927.
46. Quigley, Rev. Joseph A.M., A.B., J.C.B., Condemned Societies, 139 pp., 1927.
47. Zaplotnik, Rev. Johannes Leo, J.C.D., De Vicariis Foraneis, X-142 pp., 1927.
48. Duskie, Rev. John Aloysius, A.B., J.C.D., The Canonical Status of the Orientals in the United States, VIII-196 pp., 1928.
49. Hyland, Rev. Francis Edward, J.C.D., Excommunication, Its Nature, Historical Development and Effects, VIII-181 pp., 1928.
50. Reinmann, Rev. Gerald Joseph, O.M.C., J.C.D., The Third Order Secular of Saint Francis, 201 pp., 1928.
51. Schenk, Rev. Francis J., J.C.D., The Matrimonial Impediments of Mixed Religion and Disparity of Cult, XVI-318 pp., 1929.
52. Coady, Rev. John Joseph, S.T.D., J.U.D., A.M., The Appointment of Pastors, VIII-150 pp., 1929.
53. Kay, Rev. Thomas Henry, J.C.D., Competence in Matrimonial Procedure, VIII-164 pp., 1929.
54. Turner, Rev. Sidney Joseph, C.P., J.U.D., The Vow of Poverty, XLIX-217 pp., 1929.
55. Kearney, Rev. Raymond, A., A.B., S.T.D., J.C.D., The Principles, of Delegation, VII-149 pp., 1929.
56. Conran, Rev. Edward James, A.B., J.C.D., The Interdict, V-163 pp., 1930.
57. O'Neil, Rev. William H., J.C.D., Papal Rescripts of Favor, VII-218 pp., 1930.
58. Bastnagel, Rev. Clement Vincent, J.U.D., The Appointment of Parochial Adjutants and Assistants, XV-257 pp., 1930.
59. Ferry, Rev. William A., A.B., J.C.D., Stole Fees, V-135 pp., 1930.
60. Costello, Rev. John Michael, A.B., J.C.D., Domicile and Quasi-domicile, VII-201 pp., 1930.
61. Kremer, Rev. Michael Nicholas, A.B., S.T.B., J.C.D., Church Support in the United States, VI-1930.

62. Angulo, Rev. Luis, C.M., J.C.D., Legislation de la Iglesia sobre la intencion en la application de la Santa Misa, VII-104 pp., 1931.
63. Frey, Rev. Wolfgang Norbert, O.S.B., A.B., J.C.D., The Act of Religious Profession, VIII-174 pp., 1931.
64. Roberts, Rev. James Brendan, A.B., J.C.D., The Banns of Marriage, XIV-140 pp., 1931.
65. Ryder, Rev. Raymond Aloysius, A.B., J.C.D., Simony, IX-151 pp., 1931.
66. Campagna, Rev. Angelo, Ph.D., J.U.D., Il Vicario Generale del Vescovo, VII-205 pp., 1931.
67. Cox, Rev. Joseph Godfrey, A.B., J.C.D., The Administration of Seminaries, VI-124 pp., 1931.
68. Gregory, Rev. Donald J., J.U.D., The Pauline Privilege, XV-165 pp., 1931.
69. Donohue, Rev. John F., J.C.D., The Impediment of Crime, VII-110 pp., 1931.
70. Dooley, Rev. Eugene A., O.M.I., J.C.D., Church Law On Sacred Relics, IX-143 pp., 1931.
71. Orth, Rev. Raymond Clement, O.M.C., J.C.D., The Approbation of Religious Institutes, 171 pp., 1931.
72. Pernicone, Rev. Joseph M., A.B., J.C.D., The Ecclesiastical Prohibition of Books, XII-267 pp., 1932.
73. Clinton, Rev. Connell, A.B., J.C.D., The Paschal Precept, IX-108 pp., 1932.
74. Donnelly, Rev. Francis B., A.M., S.T.L., J.C.D., The Diocesan Synod, VIII-125 pp., 1932.
75. Torrente, Rev. Camilo, C.M.F., J.C.D., Las Processiones Sagradas, V-145 pp., 1932.
76. Murphy, Rev. Edwin J., C.PP.S., J.C.D., Suspension Ex Informata Conscientia, XI-122, pp., 1932.
77. Mackenzie, Rev. Eric F., A.M., S.T.L., J.C.D., The Delict of Heresy in its Commission Penalization, Absolution, VII-124 pp., 1932.
78. Lyons Rev. Avitus E., S.T.B., J.C.D., The Collegiate Tribunal of First Instance, XI-147 pp., 1932.
79. Connolly, Rev. Thomas A., J.C.D., Appeals, XI-195 pp., 1932.
80. Sangmeister, Rev. Joseph V., A.B., J.C.D., Force and Fear as Precluding Matrimonial Consent, V-211 pp., 1932.
81. Jaeger, Rev. Leo A., A.B., J.C.D., The Administration of Vacant and Quasi-vacant Episcopal Sees in the United States, IX-229 pp., 1932.
82. Rimlinger, Rev. Herbert T., J.C.D., Error Invalidating Matrimonial Consent, VII-79 pp., 1932.
83. Barrett, Rev. John D.M., S.S.. J.C.D., A Comparative Study of the Third Plenary Council of Baltimore and the Code, IX-221 pp., 1932.

84. Carberry, Rev. John J., Ph.D., S.T.D., J.C.D., The Juridical Form of Marriage, X-177 pp., 1934.
85. Dolan, Rev. John L., A.B., J.C.D., The Defensor Vinculi, XII-157 pp., 1934.
86. Hannan, Rev. Jerome D., A.M., S.T.D., LL.B., J.C.D., The Canon Law of Wills, IX-517 pp., 1934.
87. Lemieux, Rev. Delisle A., A.M., J.C.D., The Sentence in Ecclesiastical Procedure, IX-131 pp., 1934.
88. O'Rourke, Rev. James J., A.B., J.C.D., Parish Registers, VII-109 pp., 1934.
89. Timlin, Rev. Bartholomew, O.F.M., A.M., J.C.D., Conditional Matrimonial Consent, X-381 pp., 1934.
90. Wahl, Rev. Francis X., A.B., J.C.D., The Matrimonial Impediments of Consanguinity and Affinity, VI-125 pp., 1934.
91. White, Rev. Robert J., A.B., LL.B., S.T.B., J.C.D., Canonical Ante-Nuptial Promises and the Civil Law, VI-152 pp., 1934.
92. Herrera, Rev. Antonio Parra, O.C.D., J.C.D., Legislation Ecclesiastica sobra el Ayuno y la Abstinencia, XI-191 pp., 1935.
93. Kennedy, Rev. Edwin J., J.C.D., The Special Matrimonial Process in Cases of Evident Nullity, X-165 pp., 1935.
94. Manning, Rev. John J., A.B., J.C.D., Presumption of Law in Matrimonial Procedure, XI-111 pp., 1935.
95. Moeder, Rev. John M., J.C.D., The Proper Bishop for Ordination and Dismissorial Letters, VII-135 pp., 1935.
96. O'Mara, Rev. William A., A.B., J.C.D., Canonical Causes For Matrimonial Dispensations, IX-155 pp., 1935.
97. Reilly, Rev. Peter, J.C.D., Residence of Pastors, IX-81 pp., 1935.
98. Smith, Rev. Mariner T., O.P., S.T.L., J.C.D., The Penal Law For Religious, VII-169 pp., 1935.
99. Whalen, Rev. Donald W., A.M., J.C.D., The Value of Testimonial Evidence in Matrimonial Procedure, XIII-297 pp., 1935.
100. Cleary, Rev. Joseph F., J.C.D., Canonical Limitations on the Alienation of Church Property, VIII-141 pp., 1936.
101. Glynn, Rev. John C., J.C.D., The Promoter of Justice, XX-337 pp., 1936.
102. Brennan, Rev. James H., S.S., A.M., S.T.B., J.C.D., The Simple Convalidation of Marriage, VI-135 pp, 1937.
103. Brunini, Rev. Joseph Bernard, J.C.D., The Clerical Obligations of Canons, 139 and 142, X-121 pp., 1937.
104. Connor, Rev. Maurice, A.B., J.C.D., The Administrative Removal of Pastors, VIII-159 pp., 1937.
105. Guilfoyle, Rev. Merlin Joseph, J.C.D., Custom, XI-144 pp., 1937.
106. Hughes, Rev. James Austin, A.B., A.M., J.C.D., Witnesses in Criminal Trials of Clerics, IX-140 pp., 1937.

107. Jansen, Rev. Raymond J., A.B., S.T.L., J.C.D., Canonical Provisions for Catechetical Instruction, VII-153 pp., 1937.
108. Kealy, Rev. John James, A.B., J.C.D,, The Introductory Libellus in Church Court Procedure, XI-121 pp., 1937.
109. McManus, Rev. James Edward, C.SS.R., J.C.D., The Administration of Temporal Goods in Religious Institutes, XVI-196 pp., 1937.
110. Moriarity, Rev. Eugene James, J.C.D., Oaths in Ecclesiastical Courts, X-115 pp., 1937.
111. Rainer, Rev. Eligius George, C.SS.R., J.C.D., Suspension of Clerics, XVII-249 pp., 1937.
112. Reilly, Rev. Thomas F., C.SS.R., J.C.D., Visitation of Religious, XII-195 pp., 1938.
113. Moriarity, Rev. Francis E., C.SS.R., J.C.D., The Extraordinary Absolution from Censures, XVI-334 pp., 1938.
114. Connolly, Rev. Nicholas P., J.C.D., The Canonical Erection of Parishes, X-132 pp., 1938.
115. Donovan, Rev. James J., J.C.D., The Pastor's Obligation in Prenuptial Investigation, XII-322 pp., 1938.
116. Harrigan, Rev. Robert J., M.A., S.T.B., J.C.D., The Radical Sanation of Invalid Marriages, X-208 pp., 1938.
117. Boffa, Rev. Conrad Humbert, J.C.L., Canonical Provisions for Catholic Schools, 1939.
118. Parsons, Rev. Anscar John, O.M.Cap., J.C.L., Canonical Elections, 1939.
119. Reilly, Rev. Edward Michael, A.B., J.C.L., The General Norms of Dispensation, 1939.
120. Ryan, Rev. Gerald Aloysius, A.B., J.C.L., Principles of Episcopal Jurisdiction, 1939.

www.ingramcontent.com/pod-product-compliance
Lightning Source LLC
LaVergne TN
LVHW050225080826
844660LV00012B/474

* 9 7 8 0 8 1 3 2 2 3 0 8 7 *